CALIFORNIA

|CONDENSED|

 marisa gierlich

LONELY PLANET PUBLICATIONS
Melbourne • Oakland • London • Paris

contents

Lonely Planet Condensed – California
1st edition – April 2000

Published by
Lonely Planet Publications Pty Ltd
A.C.N. 005 607 983
192 Burwood Rd, Hawthorn,
Victoria 3122, Australia

Lonely Planet Offices
Australia PO Box 617, Hawthorn, VIC 3122
USA 150 Linden St, Oakland, CA 94607
UK 10a Spring Place, London NW5 3BH
France 1 rue du Dahomey, 75011 Paris

Photographs
All of the images in this guide are available
for licensing from Lonely Planet Images.
email: lpi@lonelyplanet.com.au

Front cover photographs
Top: Death Valley landscape
    (Richard Nebesky)
Bottom: San Francisco Museum of Modern Art
    (Richard I'Anson)

ISBN 1 86450 041 7

how to use this book

KEY TO SYMBOLS

⊠ address
☎ telephone number
🅮 email/web site address
🚇 nearest train station
🚍 nearest bus route
🚊 cable car, streetcar or trolley line
⚓ nearest ferry wharf
🚗 car access
✈ nearby airport

ⓘ tourist information
🕓 opening hours
$ cost, entry charge
♿ wheelchair access
🧒 child-friendly
✗ on-site or nearby eatery
🛏 local place to stay
V vegetarian, or with a good vegetarian selection

COLOUR-CODING

Each chapter has a different colour code which is reflected on the maps for quick reference.

MAPS & GRID REFERENCES

The fold-out maps on the front and back covers are numbered from 1 to 9. All sights and venues in the text have map references which indicate where to find them, eg (6, H4) means Map 6, grid reference H4. When a map reference appears immediately after a name, the sight is labelled on the map; when it appears after an address (eg with most restaurants, hotels etc), only the street is marked.

PRICES

Multiple prices (eg $14/10/35) indicate adult/concession/family or group entry charges. Concession prices include child, pensioner and/or student discounts. Most family tickets cover 2 adults and 2 children.

WARNING & REQUEST

Things change – prices go up, schedules change, good places go bad and bad places improve or go bankrupt. So, if you find things better or worse, recently opened or long since closed, please tell us and help make the next edition even more accurate and useful. Everyone who writes to us will find their name and possibly excerpts from their correspondence in one of our publications (let us know if you *don't* want your letter published or your name acknowledged). They will also receive the latest issue of *Planet Talk*, our quarterly printed newsletter, or *Comet*, our monthly email newsletter. Subscriptions to both newsletters are free. The very best contributions will be rewarded with a free guidebook.

Send all correspondence to the Lonely Planet office closest to you (see p. 123).

Lonely Planet books provide independent advice. Lonely Planet does not accept advertising in guidebooks, nor payment in exchange for listing or endorsing any place or business. Lonely Planet writers do not accept discounts or payments in exchange for positive coverage of any sort.

facts about california

Most people on the planet have a preconception of California, thanks to Hollywood's vast film and TV industries. What surprises many visitors is that the groovers, surfers, over-the-top mansions, Silicon Valley whizzes, silicon-enhanced bodies and spaced-out hippies are not just a product of Tinsel Town – they're all here, live and kicking.

Yet the Golden State has far more to it than the regurgitated clichés of a half-hour sitcom. The most populous and most ethnically diverse US state by far, California is a melting pot of races, cultures and subcultures. On the whole, the mix works well, though an undercurrent of tension has always brewed beneath the surface, sometimes bubbling over.

Larger than Britain and with enough road mileage to circle the globe 3 times, the state has just about every type of ecosystem in existence. Get out of the main tourist centres and you'll find parched salt flats in Death Valley, breathtaking redwood forests, serene mountain meadows and block-long towns where locals chew tobacco and swap stories about nothin' much. Outdoor activities are hugely popular, from scuba diving to ice climbing.

Californians like to be cutting edge, and for visitors it is the perfect place to check out which way-out fad will be next year's mainstream fashion or must-have technological gadget. Trends may not all start in California, but they catch on first and fastest here – from supermarkets to snowboards, hand-held computers to health-food pizzas.

Santa Monica Beach, LA, is a prime tourist hub.

HISTORY
Prehistory
Archaeological evidence, combined with accounts from early European visitors, suggests that California was home to 300,000 indigenous 'Indians', who had more than 20 language groups and 100 dialects. Conflict between the groups was almost nonexistent, and they had no class of warriors and no tradition of warfare, at least until Europeans arrived.

European Discovery
Following their conquest of Mexico in the early 1500s, the Spanish began exploring the limits of their new empire. The southern tip of California was settled in 1535, but it was not until 1539 that an exploration by Francisco de Ulloa established that it was on a peninsula rather than an island, as previously thought. The peninsula became known as Baja (Lower) California, and the coast to the north was called Alta (Upper) California.

> **The Bear Flag Republic**
> In the mid-1800s the USA made proposals to buy California from Mexico, but some settlers in northern California plotted a more direct approach. In 1845 rebels seized the town of Sonoma, hoisted an improvised flag with a crudely drawn bear and proclaimed California the 'Bear Flag Republic'. It was one of the shortest-lived republics in history, but the bear and the words 'California Republic' still survive on the state flag.

As Russian ships came to California's coast in search of sea otter pelts, and British trappers and explorers spread throughout the west, the Spanish government decided it was time for permanent settlement. Catholic missions and *presidios* (military garrisons) were the first settlements, boosted later by *pueblos* (small Spanish-style villages). Padre Junípero Serra established a mission in San Diego (1769), while Gaspar de Portola continued north and formed a second outpost at Monterey (1770). Another group came overland from Sonora, led by Juan Bautista de Anza. They settled on the San Francisco peninsula in 1776 and named the place Yerba Buena (for a 'good herb' that grew wild there). Other civilian pueblos were established at San Jose (1777) and Los Angeles (1781).

The Rancho Period
Mexico won independence from Spain in 1821. In 1833, in order to turn a profit in California, the missions were secularised, and their lands appropriated and divided between mission Indians and new settlers who were attracted by the promise of land grants.

Few Indians held on to their land as an almost feudal society, dominated by corrupt administrators and elite land-holders, developed. As American settlers in California became increasingly disaffected with the ineffectual and remote government in Mexico City, the US government's desire to control all the territory across to the Pacific grew.

Mexican-American War & Statehood

In May 1846 the USA declared war on Mexico. US forces quickly occupied all the presidios, and by 1847 they had seized Mexico City. As part of the postwar treaty, Mexico was forced to cede a huge area of land to the USA, including California. By an amazing coincidence, gold was discovered in northern California soon after the handover and over the next 2 years more than 90,000 people flooded in, boosting the population by 565%. In 1850, California was admitted to the USA as a non-slave state.

20th Century

The San Francisco earthquake and fire of 1906 destroyed most of California's largest and wealthiest city, but it was barely a hiccup in the state's ongoing development – the population increased by 60% in the decade to 1910.

The Mexican revolution (1910-21) led to huge immigrations from south of the border, and served to reinvigorate California's Hispanic heritage. WWII brought teams of military and defence workers, as well as new industries. Women were co-opted into war work, while more Mexicans came in to meet labour shortages. In the postwar boom, African Americans arrived in large numbers to fill jobs, but they were often sacked when the economy slumped. In the 1940s the population grew by 53%, and in the 50s, by another 49%.

Birth of 'The Industry'

The establishment of the movie industry in California started around 1908. Independent producers were attracted to southern California's sunny climate, which allowed indoor scenes to be shot outdoors – a boon to the unsophisticated photo technology of the day. The diverse California landscape meant ocean, desert or alpine locations were always nearby. What's more, the proximity of the Mexican border enabled filmmakers to rush their equipment to safety when challenged by the collection agents of patent holders like Thomas Edison.

California was at the forefront of the 1960s hippie counterculture, its psychedelic art, music and the new libertarianism. However, the 1968 assasination of Robert Kennedy in LA and the sometimes violent repression of demonstrations stripped that era of its innocence.

California Today

Unconstrained by the burden of tradition, bankrolled by affluence, and promoted by its pervasive media, California continues to grow. But alongside the glitz, glamour and success stories, California's urban areas are pressing the limits of traffic congestion, air pollution, water supply and available land for housing. Many Californians are concerned that the seemingly unstoppable growth may destroy the very features that make the state so attractive. Wonderful cities, beaches and national parks may be great for the economy but their development must also be sustainable.

GEOGRAPHY

The third-largest state after Alaska and Texas, California is roughly the size of Sweden, covering about 163,710 sq miles. It is bordered by Oregon to the north, Mexico to the south, Nevada and Arizona to the east, and the 700-mile Pacific coast to the west.

The main geographic regions of California are the Coastal Range (Ventura to Crescent City), the agricultural Central Valley (I-5 from LA to Sacramento), the Sierra Nevada and Cascade mountain ranges (Bakersfield to the California-Oregon border) and the vast deserts north-east of San Diego and Los Angeles (Joshua Tree to Death Valley).

Each region has its own eco-system, from low desert to alpine forest, as well as characteristic flora and fauna. California's trees include the world's tallest (coastal redwood), largest (sequoia) and oldest (bristlecone pine). It boasts one of the highest point in the US (Mt Whitney, 14, 494ft) and the lowest point (Badwater, Death Valley, 282ft *below* sea level).

> ### How Green is my Valley?
> California has always been at the fore front of environmental campaigning the Sierra Club, founded in 1892 b explorer, geologist and botanist Joh Muir, is still an active and effectiv environmental lobby group. Perhap even more 'Californian' in nature Earth First!, an eco-radical grou whose members chain themselves t old-growth trees and plant boob traps in potential logging areas.

ENVIRONMENT

California faces complex and catastrophic environmental problems. Around half of all residents live in the southern fifth of the state, in a desert environment that requires water to be 'imported' from the northern mountains. Fossil fuels are tapped for energy, wetlands and deserts are paved and built upon, freeways connect residential and work areas, and people rely heavily on cars. The population is estimated to hit 50 million by 2025.

Overgrazing and logging on the north coast threaten fish populations (namely coho salmon and steelhead trout) which, being at the base of the food chain, affects all wildlife. Ozone creeps high into the Sierra, making its pristine lakes vulnerable to acid rain and snowmelt and damaging more than 60% of its pine trees.

Despite the grim picture, California residents vigilantly fight for a cleaner state. Despite serious air-pollution, California leads the world in vehicle emission controls and environmental legislation.

Freeway upon freeway, Los Angeles

David Peevers

GOVERNMENT & POLITICS

The head of the executive branch of state government is the governor, and California's bicameral legislature consists of a 40-member senate, and an 80-member general assembly, elected for 4-year terms.

Traditionally, northern California and most urban areas, especially Los Angeles, are predominantly Democrat, while the state's rural heartland and affluent Orange and San Diego counties are Republican, in some cases conservative Republican. In the 1998 election, the state elected Gray Davis, the first Democratic governor since the late 1970s.

Current political platforms tend to focus on education and the environment. Public elementary and secondary education is commonly under-funded, and parents with sufficient income increasingly opt for private schooling, extending the gap between the haves and have-nots.

ECONOMY

If California were an independent nation, its GNP – over $22,000 per head, per year – would be the seventh-largest in the world and strongly diversified. It has the

Half Dome, Yosemite National Park

highest agricultural output in the USA, and substantial processing industries such as fish packing, fruit and vegetable packaging, wine making, petroleum processing and timber milling. Other industries include the design and production of aircraft, aerospace components, military hardware, electronics, computers and high-tech consumer goods.

Much of the economy is post-industrial, with banking, finance, education, research and development, computer software, TV, movies, tourism and corporate services all good money spinners. Real estate remains big business – in some places it seems like every second property is on the market.

Though mining was at one time California's greatest industry, it now has a minor place in the economy with most of the gold gone and the oil reserves depleted. Mining now focuses on sand, cement, gravel, borate and natural gas.

did you know?

- California produces the most solid waste, per capita, in the USA
- California's minimum wage in 1999 was $5.75 per hour
- The median price of a house on the Strand in Hermosa Beach (LA) was $42,000 in 1971; in 1999 it was $2.2 million
- Median monthly rent for a 1 bedroom apartment in The Mission (SF) was $175 in 1971; in 1999 it was $1250

SOCIETY & CULTURE

California has a population of more than 32.5 million, of the US total of around 271 million. The largest immigrant group is Mexican, followed by Filipino, Chinese, Vietnamese, Korean, Iranian and a string of other nationalities. The largest Cambodian population in the US (40,000 people) lives in Long Beach, LA. The resultant racial mix is 60% non-Hispanic white, 26% Hispanic, 7% African American and 7% 'other' (this includes 0.8% Native American).

Minority groups have often had rough treatment in California. During boom times huge numbers were sought to fill labour shortages, but when the economy slumped they were often victimised. Mexican and Latin American workers do most of the farm labour and domestic work in the state, but in 1994 Californians voted to deny illegal immigrants access to

California's diverse racial and cultural mix

state government services, including schools and hospitals. Predominantly black suburbs of LA have been the scene of violent outbursts, notably the riots of 1965, 1979 and 1992.

Still, other minority groups have flourished in California. The Gay Pride movement was born in San Francisco, and it is still the most openly, exuberantly gay city in the world.

Etiquette

California is famous for being a place where 'anything goes', but there are a few things that might attract disapproval. Dropping-in on a wave that is already being surfed by someone else is perhaps the worst social crime, and can actually lead to a fight. Running bare-chested (or in a sports-bra only) is fine on the beach or in public parks, but may draw unwanted attention in urban areas like San Francisco, Downtown LA or Sacramento. Cutting people off on the freeway is nearly a sport, but it is not appreciated nor safe. Smoking is prohibited in *all* public places.

Things that might bring good vibes include: telling people you're from out-of-state; letting cars pass if you're driving slowly; staying to one side of a busy sidewalk; and throwing garbage (including cigarette butts) in the bin.

Arts

Film California culture is unique in that the state's primary art form, film, is also a major export. It is a medium with powerful influence; as early as the 1930s, Hollywood was promoting fashions and fads for the middle classes.

The film industry was established around 1908. By 1996 it was generating more than $26 billion in revenue a year and employing around 230,000 people.

LA, in particular, has turned the camera incessantly on itself, and as a result, it's probably the most self-aware city in the world. Some fine films set in LA include: Billy Wilder's *Sunset Boulevard* (1950); Roman Polanski's *Chinatown* (1974); cult movie *Blade Runner* (1982); and crime thriller *LA Confidential* (1997).

San Francisco is home to a number of big production companies, including Francis Ford Coppola's Zoetrope and, in Marin County, LucasFilm and Industrial Light & Magic, the high-tech company that produces the computer-generated special effects for Hollywood's biggest releases.

The first big San Francisco movie was Clark Gable's *San Francisco* (1936), which relives the 1906 quake. *The Graduate* (1967), *Bullit* (1968) and *Dirty Harry* (1971) are other notable films.

Lee Foster

Life imitates art, Universal Studios

Literature Some of the brightest lights in 20th century American literature have made California their home. Hugely influential was John Steinbeck, whose novels *Grapes of Wrath* (1939) and *Cannery Row* (1945) explored the lot of the working classes.

Nathanael West's *Day of the Locust* (1939) is one of the best – and most cynical – novels about Hollywood ever written. F Scott Fitzgerald's *The Last Tycoon* (1940), and Budd Schulberg's *What Makes Sammy Run?* (1941) also dissect the early days of the film industry.

> **did you know?**
>
> The word 'California' began as a literary device – it was the name of a mythical island in a 1510 Spanish novel, *Las Sergas de Esplandan*. Spanish explorers, fancifully speculating on a golden 'island' beyond the West Coast, actually named California before it was discovered.

In the 1930s, San Francisco and Los Angeles became the capitals of the pulp detective novel. Dashiell Hammett *(The Maltese Falcon and The Thin Man)* and Raymond Chandler *(The Big Sleep)* led the way, with Jim Thompson *(The Grifters)*, Elmore Leonard *(Get Shorty)* and Walter Mosley *(Devil in a Blue Dress)* carrying on the tradition.

Beat Generation authors Jack Kerouac and Allen Ginsberg introduced a new style of writing, as did Tom Wolfe and his acid trips, while Ken Kesey took a more serious bent with *One Flew Over the Cuckoo's Nest* (1962).

Hunter S Thompson began his savage exploration of the collapse of the hippie dream with *Hell's Angels* (1970). His masterwork remains *Fear and Loathing in Las Vegas* (1971), which begins in LA.

No writer watched San Francisco's gay fraternity emerge from the closet with clearer vision than Armistead Maupin and his *Tales of the City* series.

Dance The San Francisco Bay Area is one of the best areas in the US for dance. The San Francisco Ballet, the oldest ballet company in the country, draws dancers and commissions works from all over the world. The city is also a centre for independent choreographers and modern dance companies, including ODC San Francisco, Lines Contemporary Ballet and Joe Goode Performance Group.

Music Many great jazzmen were born in Los Angeles – Dexter Gordon, Charles Mingus and Art Pepper among them. In the 1950s, Cool Jazz was developed by artists such as Dave Brubeck, Vince Guaraldi and Chet Baker.

Frank Gehry

When the shiny, undulating, explosive mass that is the Guggenheim Museum in Bilbao, Spain, opened in 1998, it brought to the world's attention the capacity of architecture and, more specifically, of an architect. But those who knew Frank Gehry's works – many of which are in LA – were not surprised. One of his best-known LA structures is the Chiat-Day Building, 340 Main St, Santa Monica (2, D1), whose entrance is through a 4-storey pair of binoculars.

David Peevers

Gehry's remarkable Chiat-Day Building

Rock 'n' roll was from the beginning recorded in California. Richie Valens, whose *La Bamba* was a rockified traditional Mexican folksong, was the first home-grown product. In the early 1960s surf music took off, spearheaded by the Beach Boys. A few years later a group of UCLA students – among them Jim Morrison – formed The Doors.

Meanwhile, San Francisco was spinning into the psychedelic revolution. Bay Area bands like Janis Joplin's Big Brother & the Holding Company, Sly & the Family Stone and Credence Clearwater Revival were key players. In the late 60s Tom Waits began haunting the smaller clubs of LA with music built on sounds dragged out from a tin pan alley junkyard.

In the late 1970s and early 80s, California Punk grew up around skateboard culture. In the late-80s, Red Hot Chili Peppers exploded on the national scene.

The area stretching from South Central LA to Long Beach is the local rap hotbed, producing such artists as Snoop Doggy Dog and NWA (Niggers With Attitude).

highlights

Calidornia's diversity ensures that its attractions satisfy a gamut of interests. Looking for a romantic getaway? Head to the Wine Country, The Redwoods region or Big Sur. Want to set out on a nature trail, plunge into sparkling waters, or bathe in sunshine? Check out Lake Tahoe, Santa Monica or Santa Catalina Island. Intrigued by the human-built oddities that seem to flourish near the Pacific? Then Hearst Castle, Venice Beach and Disneyland are the perfect modern California dream.

Not surprisingly, California's high season is summer (late May to early Sept) and that means huge crowds at all the major tourist sights. Death Valley (high season Nov-May) and Lake Tahoe (popular with skiers) are obvious exceptions. Yosemite, Kings Canyon and Sequoia national parks are beautiful in winter – practically deserted and blanketed with snow.

Most theme parks, including Disneyland, sell multi-day passes that save you quite a bit of money. It's worth checking with your hotel or motel to see if they sell discounted tickets to nearby attractions.

Suggested Itineraries

Three Days Check out the top sights of either San Francisco or LA.

One Week Four days in San Francisco (including the Wine Country or Berkeley), then fly to LA.

Two Weeks Four days in San Francisco, divert to Lake Tahoe and the Gold Country, before driving down the coast to LA and checking out Santa Catalina Island, Disneyland, then San Diego.

California Lowlights

Hollywood
Expecting a glamorous dream-world of celluloid perfection? Hollywood is all grit and grime, and actually quite depressing.

LA's Traffic
Ever since oil and tyre magnates joined forces to buy (and tear out) Los Angeles' Red Car trolley line the city's been utterly reliant on cars.

National Park crowds
Summer crowds at visitor centres can make you wonder why you tried to escape the city. Thankfully, once you hit the trails peace and quiet returns.

Sprawling Suburbs
Massive housing developments along freeways on the periphery of most major cities are using precious resources and reducing wildlife habitat.

Pollution
East of LA and north of San Diego, the cities at the foot of the beautiful San Bernardino Mountains are constantly cloaked in smog.

Blue skies and palm trees – the California dream

BALBOA PARK (9, B5)

The beautiful landscaping of San Diego's Balboa Park is attributable to horticulturalist Kate Sessions, who began transforming the area in 1892 as part of a deal with city officials.

By the turn of the century, Balboa Park had became a well-loved part of San Diego. Spanish colonial-style buildings retained from the 1915-16 Panama-California Exposition now house several museums along **El Prado**, the park's main thoroughfare.

INFORMATION

- 🚌 7, 7A, 7B from downtown
- 🚗 from downtown, take Park Blvd (12th Ave) or Cabrillo (163) Fwy; from I-5 exit at 10th Ave
- ⌚ call for times
- 💲 $21 Balboa Passport gives entry to 9 museums for 1 week; individual museums $5-7; zoo $16
- ⓘ House of Hospitality (☎ 619-239 0512), 1549 El Prado
- 📧 www.balboapark.org
- ♿ excellent
- 🍴 Sculpture Garden Cafe (San Diego Museum of Art), Albert's (at the zoo)

Tony Wheeler

The **Museum of Man** (9, A5; ☎ 619-239 2001) has artefacts from the American Southwest and excellent temporary exhibits. The **Simon Edison Center** (9, A5; ☎ 619-239 2255) has 3 theatres, including The Old Globe, which runs a popular summer Shakespeare series. The **Mingei Museum** (9, A5; ☎ 619-239 0003) has a fascinating collection of folk art from around the globe, while the **San Diego Museum of Art** (☎ 619-232 7931) has fine European paintings, American landscapes and interesting Asian galleries. The **Timken Museum of Art** (☎ 619-239 5548) houses a small but impressive collection, with paintings by Rembrandt, Rubens, El Greco and Cézanne. The **Reuben H Fleet Space Theater** (☎ 619-238 1233) shows IMAX films, while the **Natural History Museum** (☎ 619-232 3821) has good exhibits on bugs, birds, reptiles and dinosaurs. The **Aerospace Museum** (9, B5; ☎ 619-234 8291), in a building which dates from a 1935 exposition, is also interesting.

San Diego's world-class **zoo** (p. 42), at the park's northern tip, is a must.

The Botanical Building's redwood lathe protect its tropical plants from harsh su...

BIG SUR (1, G4)

An awe-inspiring experience, Big Sur is a spectacularly beautiful, sparsely populated 90-mile stretch of coastline along Hwy 1. There are no traffic lights or shopping centres, and when the sun goes down, the moon and stars are the only street lights.

Heading south from Rocky Point (1, F4), **Point Sur** is an imposing volcanic rock that looks like an island but is connected to land by a sandbar. On weekends you can tour the 1899 **Point Sur Light Station**.

Andrew Molera State Park's gentle ½-mile trail leads to a beautiful beach. From here several trails head south along the bluffs above the ocean.

If Big Sur has a hub, it is Big Sur Center (called 'the village') with the only store, post office and gas station.

Pfeiffer Big Sur State Park occupies 680 acres and has plenty of coastal hiking trails. The **Ventana Wilderness**, east of the Hwy, is popular with backpackers; Sykes Hot Springs is a favourite destination.

Housed amid gardens and sculptures, the **Henry Miller Memorial Library** has reams of the author's works and a great collection of Big Sur and Beat Generation material.

The highlight at **Julia Pfeiffer Burns State Park** is 50ft McWay Falls, which drops straight into the sea.

At Big Sur's southern edge is the **Esalen Institute**, a renowned New Age resort with expensive workshops. If that's not your scene, arrive after 11pm to enjoy the outdoor hot tubs on a cliff overlooking the ocean.

INFORMATION

- 🚌 Monterey-Salinas Transit (MST; ☎ 831-899 2555) to/from the Monterey Peninsula
- 🚗 road info ☎ 831-757 2006
- ℹ️ Ranger Station (☎ 831-667 2315), 3 miles south of Big Sur Center; *El Sur Grande* newspaper lists campgrounds, parks and businesses
- ℯ www.bigsuronline.com
- ✕ see page 80
- 🛏 see page 104

Michael Aw

DON'T MISS
- Henry Miller Memorial Library • ½-mile hike down to Partington Cove • a sunset drink at Nepenthe restaurant

Impressive viewing along Hwy 1 – Big Sur's majestic 90 miles of coastline

DEATH VALLEY   (1, G8)

The name Death Valley evokes all that is harsh, hot, and hellish – a punishing, barren, and lifeless place of Old Testament severity. Historically, the valley has not been as deadly as other parts of California, and naturalists point out that many plants and animals thrive there. Still, visitors expecting blazing sunlight, stark scenery and inhuman scale will not be disappointed.

The valley itself is about 100 miles long, and 5-15 miles wide, with the Panamint Range on its west side and the Amargosa Range on its east side. **Death Valley National Park** (1, F7) covers a much larger area, and includes several other ranges and valleys to the north. It's not hard to find your way around the valley by car; there are only a few main roads and they're all well marked. **Furnace Creek**, 12 miles south of the junction of Hwys 190 and 374, has most of the visitor facilities.

Dante's View has the best overall view of the valley; it's absolutely brilliant at sunrise. Down toward the central valley, **Zabriskie Point** is another good sunrise/sunset spot. In the park's north is **Scotty's Castle** (☎ 760-786 2392), the Spanish-Moorish mansion built in the 1920s by Walter E Scott (aka 'Death Valley Scotty') for Chicago insurance magnate Albert Johnson. **Eureka Sand Dunes**, an arduous but recommended side trip west from Scotty's Castle, rise up to 680ft from a dry lake-bed.

Back down in the valley is the scenic loop at Mesquite Flat Sand Dunes and the nearby Stovepipe Wells village. A few miles south-west, the valley floor is filled with lumps of crystallised salt, aptly called **Devil's Golf Course**.

INFORMATION

- good roads from every direction
- $10/car; valid 7 days
- Furnace Creek Visitor Center (☎ 760-786 2331; 8am-5pm); 24hr ranger assistance ☎ 760-786 2330
- www.nps.gov/deva; www.deathvalley.com
- Furnace Creek Ranch
- Furnace Creek Resort (☎ 760-786 2345; www.furnacecreek resort.com), Stovepipe Wells Village (☎ 760-786 2387)

Marisa Gierlich

DON'T MISS

- Dante's View • Zabriskie Point • Twenty Mule Team Canyon
- Ubehebe Crater • Mesquite Flat Sand Dunes

At 3 million acres, Death Valley is the largest national park in the continental US.

DISNEYLAND   (1, J7)

Opened in 1955 by Walt Disney, Disneyland is billed as the 'happiest place on earth'. From the impeccable, pastel-coloured sidewalks to the incessantly grinning park employees (known as 'cast members'), Disneyland is the centrepiece of a mammoth corporate success that started with a cartoon mouse in 1928.

You can see the entire park in a day, but it requires 2 or 3 days to go on all the rides, especially in summer when queues are long. Visiting midweek is usually less hectic and arriving early in the day is best. You can avoid the ticket line crush by buying your ticket at the Disneyland Hotel and riding the monorail into the park.

You enter Disneyland on **Main Street USA**, which is a cheery re-creation of small-town America circa 1900. This is where you're most likely to find jumbo Disney characters hanging out. The park is divided into 4 different 'lands', centred around **Sleeping Beauty's Castle**, a big pink palace inspired by Germany's Neuschwanstein palace.

Fantasyland has rides based on Disney characters, while jungle-themed **Adventureland** is home to the Indiana Jones adventure. **Frontierland** has Western-style attractions, including Big Thunder

INFORMATION

- ✉ 1313 Harbor Blvd, Anaheim
- ☎ 714-999 4565
- 🚉 Amtrak from LA's Union station
- 🚌 Airport Bus (☎ 800-772 5299) from LA airport to Anaheim hotels every ½ hr; Greyhound to/from LA and San Diego
- 🚗 I-5 to Ball Rd exit, turn right into West St, continue ¼ mile to car park ($8)
- 🕐 Mon-Fri 10am-6pm; weekends, holidays 9am-midnight
- 💲 $38/28 (1 day)
- ℹ Visitor's Bureau (☎ 714-999 8999; www.anaheimoc.org), 800 W Katella Ave
- 🌐 www.disneyland.com
- ♿ good
- 🛏 Disneyland Hotel (☎ 714-778 6600); Disneyland Pacific Hotel (☎ 714-999 0990)

Stuart Wasserman

'etty in pink – Sleeping Beauty's Castle

Mountain (a roller coaster through an Old West mining town). **Tomorrowland**, the park's high-tech showpiece, offers Space Mountain, Star Tours, and the 3-D film *Captain EO*, starring Michael Jackson. **Mickey's Toontown** is a recent addition; its wacky buildings make the rest of the park look 'normal'.

DOWNTOWN LOS ANGELES   (3)

Perennial doubters and incorrigible cynics will never believe it, but LA *does* have a centre – Downtown. Few areas of LA have as much to offer per square mile – it's rich in history (as the city's birthplace), architecture, restaurants and cultural institutions.

The **Civic Center** (3, E3) contains the most important of LA's city, county, state and federal office buildings, the most distinctive of which is the 1928 **City Hall** (3, E4), which served as the 'Daily Planet' building in *Superman* and the police station in *Dragnet*. The trio of theatres – Dorothy Chandler Pavilion, Ahmanson and

Central Library's impressive skylit interi

Mark Taper Forum – that make up the **Music Center of LA County** (p. 85) are to be joined by the Disney Symphony Hall, the future home of the LA Philharmonic, in 2001.

Much of LA's modern financial district sits atop historic **Bunker Hill** (3, F3), once a fashionable neighbourhood flecked with stately Victorian mansions. The area is reached via **Angels Flight** – built in 1901 as 'the shortest railway in the world' – or the **Bunker Hill Steps**, LA's answer to Rome's Spanish Steps. At its base you'll find the **Westin Bonaventure Hotel** (3, F2), whose quintet of cylindrical glass towers has been in many TV shows and movies, the acclaimed **Museum of Contemporary Art** (p. 34), and **LA Central Library** (p. 35).

On the corner of 3rd and Broadway is the 1917 **Grand Central Market** (p. 63), a bustling food bazaar crammed with stalls selling herbs, spices, cheeses, candy and fresh produce. Across the street at 304 Broadway is the elegant **Bradbury Building** (p. 34).

South of here, Broadway becomes a vibrant Latino retail hub. The stretch between 5th St and Olympic Blvd is also a **National Register Historic District**; most impressive of the buildings are the movie palaces (p. 36) built from 1913-31.

Heading west is **Pershing Square**, LA's oldest public park (1886), and the **Biltmore Hotel** (3, G3) on Olive St, one of LA's grandest. It has hosted presidents, the 1960 Democratic National Convention and 8 Academy Awards ceremonies.

Extending south-east from Broadway, the **Garment District** (3, J4) has been a manufacturing centre and paradise of wholesale clothing since the 1930s.

The heart of **El Pueblo de Los Angeles**, the 1781 founding site of LA, is **Olvera St** (3, D4), a narrow, block-long passageway that's been an open-air Mexican marketplace since 1930. The street is home to LA's oldest building, the refurbished **Avila Adobe** (1808), built by a wealthy Mexican ranchero who became LA's mayor in 1810. Sepulveda House (☎ 213-628 1274), 622 N Main St, is the historic area's information hub.

Nearby **Union Station** (3, D4), built in 1939, is the last of the great railroad stations in the US. Its impressive marble-floored waiting room is decked with massive original chandeliers and elegant leather armchairs.

Contrasts of Downtown: life and art amid the traffic and skyscrapers

North-east of the Pueblo, LA's **Chinatown** (3, C3) is home to less than 5% of LA's 200,000 Chinese, yet the district is clearly a social and cultural hub. Dozens of restaurants and shops line the streets and in passages like Bamboo Lane (3, B3), you'll find traditional acupuncturists and herbalists.

The streets and outdoor shopping centres of **Little Tokyo** (3, F4) are flush with sushi bars, bento houses and traditional Japanese gardens.

DON'T MISS • the Westin Bonaventure Hotel's cocktail lounge • Geffen Contemporary Museum • the *Los Angeles Times* building (p. 35)

GETTY CENTER (2, B1)

One of LA's newest attractions, the Getty Center hunkers atop a Brentwood hillside like an impregnable postmodern fortress. Billions of dollars and 14yrs in the making, the 110 acre 'campus' unites the art collections assembled by the oil magnate J Paul Getty with several Getty-sponsored institutes focused on conservation, art research and education.

INFORMATION

- ✉ 1200 Getty Center Dr, Brentwood
- ☎ 310-440 7300
- 🚆 LA Metro 561 & SM Big Blue Bus 14
- 🚗 exit at Getty Center Dr from the San Diego (405) Fwy; parking reservations ($5) required 1 week in advance
- ⏰ Tues-Wed 11am-7pm, Thur-Fri 11am-9pm, Sat-Sun 10am-6pm
- $ free
- 🅴 www.getty.edu
- ♿ excellent
- ✕ 2 cafes (lunch); The Restaurant (☎ 310-440 7300) for lunch & dinner; booking required

David Peevers

The centre in no way resembles the small museum of Greek and Roman antiquities, 18th-century French furniture and European paintings that Getty created at his Malibu home in 1953. Designed by Richard Meier, this monumental cluster of massive white edifices is oddly a very welcoming place once you get up close. Nevertheless, the building has been the focus of much political, ethical and architectural debate.

On view in 4 two-storey pavilions is the museum's permanent collection; a fifth pavilion has changing exhibits. While the sky-lit galleries on the upper floors focus on European paintings, the lower floors are given over to sculpture, illuminated manuscripts, drawings, furniture, photography, glass, ceramics and other decorative arts. The garden, designed by Robert Irwin, is one of the most appealing features. Tours, lectures and the latest interactive technology make it all very accessible.

Getty Better all the Time

The Getty institutes, administered from the Getty Center, are diverse and exceedingly well endowed. Some of the areas they tackle include: conservation research and field projects; global networks for research, education and enjoyment; arts education in American schools; and educational programs for museum professionals. The Getty Grant Program has, since its inception in 1984, awarded over $82 million to more than 2,000 projects.

The centre's sensually curved buildings are juxtaposed with geometric ones, creating a remarkable play of light and shade when the sun's out.

GOLDEN GATE BRIDGE & PARK   (6)

The beautiful **Golden Gate Bridge**, almost 2 miles long with a main span of 4200ft, links San Francisco with Marin County. At the time of completion (1937) it was the longest suspension bridge in the world. Its name comes from the nickname early visitors gave to the harbour's entrance, but its actual colour is 'international orange'. Painting the bridge is a never-ending task; a team of 25 painters adds another 1000 gallons every week.

Pedestrians and cyclists can cross the bridge for free; cars pay a $3 toll for south-bound travel.

Fort Point Lookout (6, H1) offers some of the most spectacular views of the bridge and an impressive example of its 3ft-thick suspension cable. Another dramatic view is from **Lands End** (6, K3), while the lookout from **Vista Point** on the north side presents San Francisco as the bridge's backdrop.

Golden Gate Park (6, J4) is the city's biggest. Besides gardens, lakes, sporting facilities and trails, it's home to a variety of museums and open-air performance venues. The **California Academy of Sciences** (7, K1) is home to the Steinhart Aquarium and Morrison Planetarium. The **MH de Young Memorial Museum** (6, H4) has a fine collection of American art while the adjacent **Asian Art Museum** has superb pieces from the Middle East, India,

and Asia. It's claimed fortune cookies were invented at the **Japanese Tea Garden** in 1909. The 70-acre **Strybing Arboretum & Botanical Gardens** (6, H4) includes a fragrance garden, native plant collection and the Japanese Moon-Viewing Garden. On Sunday, John F Kennedy Parkway (the main thoroughfare) is closed to vehicles in the name of outdoor recreation – rent bikes or skates on Stanyan St (7, J2).

INFORMATION

- 🚍 Muni 28, 29, 43 to bridge & park
- 🕐 most park museums 9am-5pm
- 💲 $10 Culture Pass gives entry to all Golden Gate Park attractions, valid over several days
- ℹ️ Fort Point Visitors Center (☎ 415-556 1693) runs candle-light tours Nov-Feb; McLaren Lodge (☎ 415-831 2700) for info in the park
- 🅔 www.nps.gov/fopo (bridge); www.sanfranciscoonline.com (park)
- ♿ excellent at Golden Gate Park; lower level of Fort Point only

John Elk III

A vital transport link and monumental landmark, the bridge is almost 2 miles long.

HEARST CASTLE   (1, G4)

Perched high on a hill overlooking vast pastureland and the Pacific Ocean, Hearst Castle is a monument to wealth and ambition. Built by legendary newspaper magnate William Randolph Hearst, the house – La Cuesta Encantada (The Enchanted Hill) – was modelled on a Mediterranean village.

The castle sprawls over 127 acres of lushly landscaped gardens, accentuated by shimmering pools, fountains and statues from ancient Greece and Moorish Spain. The 165 rooms in 4 houses are furnished with Italian and Spanish antiques and enhanced by 41 fireplaces and 61 bathrooms. There's a private 'cathedral', a zoo and numerous entertainment rooms. Construction began on the house in 1919 but the project was never fully finished as the power-obsessed Hearst continually demanded new wings, buildings and exhibition spaces be built to accommodate his new purchases.

Hearst's art collection was so vast that an accurate calculation of its size or value was never possible. The display of wealth borders on grotesque and the amalgam of styles and periods is enough to make any architect or historian grimace. But it's well worth the entry fee to witness this American attempt at becoming 'royal' and visit the subterranean pool where Errol Flynn and his ilk dallied.

INFORMATION

- ✉ 750 Hearst Castle Rd, San Simeon
- ☎ 805-927 6811
- 🚌 off Hwy 1, 10 miles north of Cambria
- 🕐 by tour only from 8.20am-3.20pm (4.20pm in summer)
- 💲 $14/8 (under 6s free)
- ℹ tours start at the Visitor Center (be sure to book; ☎ 800-444 4445)
- 🌐 www.hearstcastle.org
- ♿ excellent; ☎ 805-927 2020 for tours
- 🍴 cafeteria at the Visitor Center
- 🛏 San Simeon Lodge (☎ 805-927 4601), 9520 Castillo Dr; Silver Surf Motel (☎ 805-927 4661, 800-621 3999), 9390 Castillo Dr

did you know?

When Hearst died in 1951 the castle was left to his heirs, but they offered the insanely high-maintenance property to the University of California. They too rejected it, and the state took it over as a museum.

The Neptune Pool; playground of the rich and famous

Richard Nebesky

Marisa Gierlich

KINGS CANYON & SEQUOIA NATIONAL PARKS   (1, F6)

On the Sierra Nevada's western slope, the adjacent Kings Canyon and Sequoia national parks encompass some of California's finest alpine scenery, as well as groves of giant sequoia trees. The 2 parks are run as 1 unit; the main visitor centres of **Grant Grove** and **Lodgepole** are on the Generals Hwy, which weaves through the parks' south-west.

Designed primarily as hiking and backpacking parks, they have few drive-by sites but loads of trails for all abilities.

At 8200ft, Kings Canyon National Park's awesome **canyon** is the deepest in the lower 48 states. At its western end multi-hued rock slopes down to the river in chunks and blade-like ridges.

Sequoia National Park's oldest tree, the **General Grant Tree**, is estimated to be more than 3500 years old, while the massive **General Sherman Tree**, in Giant Forest, is the largest (known) living tree on earth. **Redwood Mountain Grove**, about 6 miles south of Grant Grove, has the park's most extensive concentration of sequoia

INFORMATION

- ✉ 47050 Generals Hwy, Three Rivers
- 🚌 Hwy 180 from Fresno to Grant Grove, Hwy 198 to Ash Mountain
- 💲 $10/car, $5/pedestrian; valid 7 days
- ℹ visitor centres: Grant Grove (☎ 209-335 2856), Lodgepole (☎ 209-565 3782), Ash Mountain (☎ 209-565 3132), Cedar Grove (☎ 209-565 3793); recorded information ☎ 559-565 3341
- 🌐 www.nps.gov/seki
- ✗ several throughout the parks
- 🛏 reserve through Kings Canyon Park Service (☎ 209-335 5000) or, in Sequoia, DNPS (☎ 407-452 2121/3043)

trees. Also worth seeing is **Crystal Cave**, which has formations thought to be 10,000 years old. Tours of the cave ($5) can be organised at the Lodgepole or Ash Mountain visitor centres.

Several **walking trails** are accessible from Generals Hwy, while Lands End (a few miles west of Cedar Grove) and Mineral King (in the southern part of Sequoia NP) offer the best wilderness access.

Lee Foster

GENERAL SHERMAN

...equoias usually die from toppling over; ...r shallow root system struggles to support their mammoth weight.

LAKE TAHOE (1, D5)

Brilliantly blue and totally surrounded by mountains, Lake Tahoe is one of California's best destinations for those who like outdoor activities and entertainment. The California-Nevada state line cuts lengthwise through the lake, so the eastern shore (especially **Stateline**) has casinos, glitzy resorts and 'chapels' where you can get married in 15 minutes for $45. The west shore is a totally different scene, with 'towns' – **Meeks Bay, Tahoma, Homewood** and **Sunnyside** – which are little more than gatherings of cabins and woodsy resorts. Here you'll also find some of the prettiest sections of the lake – notably Rubicon Point and Lester beach at **DL Bliss State Park**. At the south-west corner of the lake, **Emerald Bay** is a shade of green that is truly spectacular.

On the north shore, **Tahoe City** is the lake's second largest hub and has been its primary boating community since Italian and Portuguese fishermen settled there in the 1860s. The Truckee River is Lake Tahoe's only outlet; it flows from Tahoe City to the historic mining town of **Truckee,** where restored buildings house shops, restaurants and plenty of bars. Skiers have choices on all sides – there are 14 downhill resorts, 6 cross-country areas and unlimited wilderness possibilities. Mountain bikers will not want to miss the Marlette Flume Trail and backpackers should explore the Desolation Wilderness area.

INFORMATION

- 🚊 Amtrak to/from Sacramento & Reno (Nevada) to Truckee
- 🚌 Tahoe Area Rapid Transit (TART) connects towns around the lake; Greyhound and Amtrak from Stateline to Sacramento & SF
- 🚗 180 miles east of SF, via I-80; road conditions ☎ 800-266 2883
- ℹ️ South Lake Tahoe (☎ 530-541 5255); North Lake Tahoe (☎ 530-583 3494); Truckee Donner (☎ 530-587 0476); Truckee Ranger Station (☎ 530-587 3558)
- ℮ www.laketahoe.com
- ✕ The Bridgetender (Tahoe City); Sunnyside Lodge, Stony Ridge Cafe (west shore)
- 🛏️ plenty in Stateline; reservation agencies: North Tahoe (☎ 800-824 6348), Squaw Valley (☎ 800-545 4350); South Lake Tahoe (☎ 800-698 2463)

Spectacular Emerald Bay

Lee Foster

THE REDWOODS REGION   (1, B2)

Coastal redwoods *(Sequoia sempervirens)*, found in a narrow 450-mile strip along the Pacific Coast from central California to southern Oregon, grow nowhere else on earth. These towering beauties, named for the colour of their wood and bark, can live up to 2200 years, grow to 367.8ft (the tallest tree ever recorded) and achieve a diameter of 22ft at the base. Standing on the needle-padded floor of a redwood forest, surrounded by silence and inhaling that fresh woody scent, is easily akin to a religious experience.

The 80-sq-mile **Humboldt Redwoods State Park** (1, C2) holds some of the world's most magnificent old-growth redwood forest. Highlights include the awe-inspiring Founders Grove, Rockefeller Grove and the Avenue of the Giants, a 32-mile stretch of scenic highway. Between **Eureka** (hub of California's northern coast) and the Oregon border, 4 parks, all with spectacular redwood groves, are managed cooperatively as the Redwood National & State Parks. **Redwood National Park's** (1, B2) Tall Trees Grove has several of the world's tallest trees. **Prairie Creek Redwoods State Park** (1, B2) features the beautiful Fern Canyon, miles of wild and untouched coastline and herds of large Roosevelt elk. **Del Norte Redwoods State Park** (1, A2) has magnificent tidal pools, and **Jedediah Smith Redwoods State Park** (1, A2), a few miles inland at the confluence of the Smith River and Mill Creek, is often sunny when the coast is cloaked in fog.

INFORMATION

✉ Hwy 101, from Garberville to the Oregon border

🚌 Greyhound to/from SF; Redwood Transit System (☎ 707-443 0826) services the local area

🚗 6hrs north of SF

✈ Arcata-Eureka airport; flights to/from SF

💲 state parks free; Redwood National Park $10

ⓘ Redwood National & State Parks Info Center (☎ 707-488 3461), Hwy 101, 1 mile south of Orick; Humboldt Redwoods Visitor Center (☎ 707-946 2263), Avenue of the Giants just south of Weott

🌐 www.treesofmystery .net; www.nps.gov/ redw

✗ plenty in Garberville, Crescent City & Klamath; for Eureka, see page 80

🛏 Miranda Gardens Resort (☎ 707-943 3011) and Historic Myers Inn (☎ 707-943 3259), both on the Avenue of the Giants; for Eureka see page 104

Try some tree-hugging therapy

Lee Foster

MONTEREY PENINSULA (1, F3)

Spectacular coastal scenery, a colourful history as the old Spanish and Mexican capital of California, a world-famous aquarium, and an abundance of private wealth all come together on the Monterey Peninsula, which juts into the Pacific Ocean on California's Central Coast.

INFORMATION

🚌 Greyhound from LA & SF; Monterey-Salinas Transit (MST; ☎ 831-899 2555) south to Big Sur

✈ Monterey Peninsula airport; direct flights to/from SF & LA

ⓘ Monterey Visitors Center (☎ 835-649 1770), cnr Camino El Estero & Del Monte Ave; *Coast Weekly* has 'what's on' listing

🌐 www.monterey.com

✕ see page 81

🛏 see page 105

Lee Foster

Michael Aw

In amongst the fish, Monterey Bay Aquarium

Monterey Bay, protected as a National Marine Sanctuary, is one of the world's richest and most varied marine environments. Highlights are its famous kelp forests, and mammals such as sea otters, seals, sea lions, elephant seals, dolphins and whales.

The spectacularly scenic **17-Mile Drive** links the peninsula's main townships, Carmel and Monterey, passing the million-dollar homes of **Pebble Beach** on the way.

Nowhere is California's Latino heritage richer than in **Monterey**, which abounds in lovingly restored old adobe (sun-dried brick) buildings. **Monterey State Historic Park**, near the water just north of downtown, encompasses 6 of Monterey's finest historic buildings. These include **Stevenson House**, formerly the French Hotel, where Robert Louis Stevenson reputedly wrote *Treasure Island*, and the **Maritime Museum of Monterey**, which has a great ship-in-a-bottle collection. The park's visitor centre, 20 Custom House Plaza, has free brochures and a detailed booklet.

In its heyday, **Cannery Row** was the hectic and smelly home of Monterey's sardine trade, a highly profitable industry from 1926-45. Nowadays, Cannery Row is a tacky 7-block enclave of restaurants and souvenir shops – a world away from the place depicted in John Steinbeck's famous novel of the same name. Its one redeeming feature is **Monterey Bay Aquarium** (☎ 800-756 3737; 10am-6pm); the wonderful Kelp Forest lets you view sharks and other creatures swimming between towering fronds of kelp.

Like Cannery Row, **Fisherman's Wharf** is just a tourist trap at heart, but it's fun nevertheless. It has a plentiful supply of restaurants, regular visits by noisy seals, and is the base for a variety of boat trips, including whale-watching expeditions.

A couple of km west of Monterey is the relaxed resort of **Pacific Grove**, famous for its winter population of monarch butterflies. Just past Pacific Grove, at the northern tip of the Monterey Peninsula, is the 1855 **Point Piños Lighthouse**. It's open on weekends only, 1-4pm.

Carmel-by-the-Sea, which began as a planned seaside resort in the 1880s, had already established a reputation as a slightly bohemian retreat by the early 1920s. The artistic flavour survives (actor Clint Eastwood is a former mayor), though Carmel is now thoroughly affluent. The town's picturesque appearance is ensured by local bylaws that forbid street lights, sidewalks and, in the central area, letterboxes. Even phone booths and newspaper vending machines are covered in shingles to keep the town's aesthetic seamless. Attractions include a neat grid of picturesque homes, an impressive coastal frontage and an upscale shopping street (where chewing gum and ice cream are prohibited). A beautiful Spanish mission, **San Carlos Borromeo del Rio Carmelo**, is just south of town, at 3080 Rio Rd, off Hwy 1. Built in 1771, the mission (☎ 831-624 1271) is open 9.30am-4.30pm, till 7.30pm in summer.

Point Lobos State Reserve, 4 miles south of Carmel, offers a good selection of short walks and some nice scuba diving. **Devil's Cauldron**, a blowhole and whirlpool that gets splashy at high tide, is also popular.

DON'T MISS
- Monterey Bay Aquarium • Monterey State Historic Park
- monarch butterflies • San Carlos Borromeo del Rio Carmelo

Monterey Bay's appealing coastline attracts all forms of wildlife.

John Elk III

SANTA CATALINA ISLAND   (1, J6)

Santa Catalina is one of the largest of the Channel Islands, a chain of semi-submerged mountains offshore between Santa Barbara and San Diego. The only island with a year-round population (3000) and sizeable tourism industry, Catalina (as it's called by locals) is only 1hr by boat from LA – a piece of paradise that makes for a lovely day trip.

INFORMATION

- Catalina Express (☎ 310-519 1212) and Catalina Cruises (☎ 800-228 2546) to/from Long Beach & San Pedro (LA Harbor)
- ① Visitor Bureau (☎ 310-510 1520) on Green Pier; organised tours see page 58
- ℮ www.catalina.com
- ✗ Cafe Prego (Italian); Armstrong's (fish)
- ⛴ Pavillion Lodge (☎ 800-851 0217), in the heart of town close to the beach; Inn at Mt Ada (☎ 310-510 2030), Old Wrigley Mansion, 398 Wrigley Rd

'Discovered' by the Spanish in 1542, Catalina remained relatively untouched until 1811, when the native seafaring Indians were forced to resettle on the mainland. In 1919 the island was bought by William Wrigley Jr (heir to the chewing-gum fortune), who built a mansion and an art deco **casino** there.

The Mediterranean-flavoured port town of **Avalon**, which has attracted tourists since the 1930s, is the only town. Most of its buildings were built in the 1920s and are decorated with colourful Catalina tile, made on the island from 1927-37. North-west of Avalon, where the island pinches together at an isthmus, **Two Harbors** gets the majority of private boat traffic and can be visited as a day trip from Avalon. The remainder of the island's coastline is undeveloped. Its rugged interior supports 400 species of indigenous plants, over 100 types of birds and numerous animals including deer, goats, boar and several hundred bison descended from those shipped over for the filming of Zane Grey's *The Vanishing American* in 1925. Offshore, extremely clear water, abundant marine life and giant kelp forests make excellent snorkelling and scuba diving territory.

The Santa Catalina Island Conservancy bought 86% of the island from the Wrigley family in 1975, thus (hopefully) ensuring its preservation from future big development.

Colourful Catalina tile decorates the Mediterranean-flavoured port town of Avalon.

SANTA MONICA & VENICE (2, D1)

With its lovely pier, pedestrian-friendly downtown and colourful shopping precincts, Santa Monica is one of the best parts of LA.

The heart of Santa Monica is the **Third St Promenade**, a pedestrian mall that extends for 3 long blocks from Wilshire Blvd south to Broadway. Here you'll find street entertainment (especially on weekends), restaurants, bars and movie theatres. **Palisades Park**, perched on a bluff overlooking the Pacific, offers unparalleled sunset views. At the park's south end is the famous **Santa Monica Pier**, with restaurants, bars, shops and a 1920s carousel featured in the movie *The Sting*.

Worth checking out are the **Santa Monica Museum of Art** (☎ 310-453 7535; Wed-Sun 11am-6pm) at Bergamot Station, 2525 Michigan Ave, and the excellent **Museum of Flying** (☎ 310-392 8822; Wed-Sun 10am-5pm), 2772 Donald Douglas Loop North.

Santa Monica's **Main St**, flanked with boutiques and hip eateries, runs south for 2 miles until it enters the

INFORMATION

🚌 Tide Shuttle to/from Santa Monica Visitors Center & Downtown LA; MTS 4 & 20 run 24hrs to/from Downtown

ⓘ Santa Monica Visitors Center (☎ 310-393 7593), 1400 Ocean Ave (in a kiosk in Palisades Park)

ⓔ www.venicebeach .com; www.venice.net

✕ Jodi Maroni's Sausage Kingdom (Ocean Front Walk) and Bamboo (p. 73) in Venice; Schatzi on Main and Chinois on Main (p. 73) in Santa Monica

community of Venice at Rose Ave. Venice's chief attraction is **Ocean Front Walk** – or, more specifically, the slice of life that hangs out there. Along its 1 mile stretch you'll see jugglers, musicians, tarot readers, bikini-clad body builders at Muscle Beach and basketball players. This scene is best explored by foot, as weekend parking is nightmarish and crowds can make bike riding and roller skating treacherous.

David Peevers

...t all traffic congestion is caused by cars.

WINE COUNTRY (5, A3)

According to local lore, the Wine Country got its start in 1857, when Hungarian Count Agoston Haraszthy purchased a defunct vineyard in Sonoma. The region really took off in 1976, when 2 Napa Valley wines – Château Montelena's 1973 chardonnay and Stag's Leap's 1973 cabernet sauvignon – outscored the French wines in a blind tasting in Paris.

Lee Foster

INFORMATION

🚌 Greyhound from SF to Calistoga via St Helena; Golden Gate Transit 90 from SF (Transbay Terminal) to Sonoma; Sonoma County Transit (☎ 707-576 7433, 800-345 7433) services Sonoma Valley

🚗 Hwy 101 to the Hwy 37 exit, then Hwy 121 to the junction with Hwy 12; take Hwy 12 north for Sonoma, or head east for Napa

ⓘ Napa Valley Visitors Bureau (☎ 707-226 4759), 1310 Napa Town Center; Sonoma Valley Visitors Bureau (☎ 707-935 4747), Viansa Winery, 25200 Arnold Dr

🌐 www.napavalley.com; www.sonoma.com

✕ see page 82

🛏 see page 106

These days the parallel Sonoma and Napa valleys are home to more than 240 wineries, with 75 or so in less famous but equally fertile neighbouring valleys. Only about 5% of California wine comes from the Wine Country, but it is generally the top 5%.

There are more than 200 wineries in the 30-mile **Napa Valley**, and most are open for tastings from 11am-4.30pm (usually $3 for 3 varieties). **Napa**, at the valley's southern end, is the major town but of little interest. Better places for a pause are **St Helena** (1, D3), with its fantastic Silverado Museum on Library Lane, and, at the top of the valley, **Calistoga** (1, D3), known for its spas and mineral water. A popular way to explore the valley is on the **Napa Valley Wine Train** (☎ 707-253 2111, 800-427 4124), a 1915 Pullman dining car that travels from Napa to St Helena and back. It does lunch, dinner or a champagne brunch on weekends.

Sonoma Valley, with its 40 or so family-owned wineries and

Labour of love – tending to the vines in the Sonoma Valley

Grapevines at Benziger Winery, Sonoma Valley

quiet rural back roads, is much more appealing than the somewhat sterile Napa Valley. **Sonoma**, at the valley's southern end, is surrounded by vineyards and has a fascinating history as the site of the 1846 Bear Flag Republic uprising (see page 6). Worth seeing is historic **Sonoma Plaza**, laid out by Mexican general Mariano Vallejo in 1834.

The best times to visit the Wine Country are during autumn, when the grapes are on the vine, or in spring, when the hills are a brilliant green hue. The Wine Country can be covered on a hectic day trip from San Francisco, but to do it justice, allow 2 full days. See page 58 for organised tours to the area.

Top Tipples

Clos Pegase Winery
✉ 1060 Dunaweal La, Calistoga
☎ 707-942 4981

Domaine Chandon
✉ 1 California Dr, west of St Helena Hwy, Yountville ☎ 707-944 2280

Hess Collection & Winery
✉ 4411 Redwood Rd, Napa
☎ 707-255 1144

Sebastiani Vineyards
✉ 389 4th St E, Sonoma ☎ 707-938 5532

St Supéry
✉ 8440 St Helena Hwy, Rutherford
☎ 707-942 3344

Architecture, art and wine come together at Calistoga's Clos Pegase Winery.

YOSEMITE NATIONAL PARK   (1, E5)

A place of ravishing natural beauty, Yosemite National Park encompasses vast and diverse landscapes which are a boon to walkers, hikers, trekkers, rock climbers, skiers and nature lovers.

The first national park in the world (1890) thanks to the passionate campaigning of naturalist John Muir, Yosemite is now one of the most visited spots in the USA, attracting 4.1 million tourists a year. On arrival it can seem brutally crowded, but you need only hit the trails to find solitude and wilderness.

The park's tourist hub is **Yosemite Valley**, where most of the facilities and campgrounds are based. The valley's epicentre, **Yosemite Village**, has a visitor centre, post office, restaurants and several museums. The valley's famous glacier-swept panorama, with **Half Dome** cliff on one side and **El Capitan** (a 3593ft granite monolith) on the other, is truly breathtaking.

West of Yosemite Village there's an easy path to the base of **Yosemite Falls**, which, at 2425ft, is the highest waterfall in North America. One of the park's best views is from **Glacier Point**, 3214ft above the valley floor, while **Valley View Turnout** on the other side of the valley is the best place to ogle El Capitan.

Tuolumne Meadows' wide open fields and clear blue lakes are a dazzling contrast to Yosemite's densely forested valley. Access it via Tioga Rd (Hwy 120), which also offers excellent day hikes.

INFORMATION

- 🚃 Amtrak to Merced depot (☎ 209-722 6862), then VIA bus (☎ 209-384 1315) to Yosemite
- 🚌 Greyhound to Merced depot, VIA to Yosemite
- 🚗 Hwy 41 from Fresno, Hwy 140 from Merced or Hwy 120 from SF
- 💲 $20/car, $10/pedestrian; valid 7 days
- ℹ️ Yosemite Valley Visitors Center (☎ 209-372 0299); info stations at Big Oak Flat, Wawona and Tuolumne Meadows (summer only); road/weather conditions ☎ 209-372 0200
- 📧 www.nps.gov/yose
- 🍴 plenty in Yosemite Village & Curry Village
- 🛏️ book through Yosemite Concession Services (☎ 209-252 4848)

Richard I'Anson

Tuolumne Meadows is the largest sub-alpine meadow in the Sierra Nevada.

sights & activities

LOS ANGELES

A sprawling urban patchwork of historic and trendy suburbs, the 467-sq-mile City of LA (population 3.68 million) comprises only a fraction of LA County (population 9.5 million), which encompasses more than 80 cities. Travellers would be wise to base themselves in a largely self-contained area – Santa Monica, Venice, West Hollywood – and rent a car; the freeways are as integral to LA living as sunshine and Mexican food.

Despite the perception that LA has no centre, **Downtown** (p. 18) is the city's historic and cultural hub, full of interesting architecture and great eateries. Nearby **Hollywood** is largely a place of nostalgia. No trip to LA would be complete without walking along the Hollywood Walk of Fame (p. 52), or comparing hand and foot prints with those at Mann's Chinese Theater (p. 36).

Beverly Hills lives up to its TV myth, with its winding, tree-lined streets and lavish estates of the rich and famous. The designer shopping mecca of **Rodeo Drive** is a great place to dream or buy.

One of LA's hippest neighbourhoods, **West Hollywood** teems with nightclubs, restaurants and elegant hotels. Numerous galleries add an artsy touch, boutique shops on **Melrose Ave** cater to fashion slaves and the **Sunset Strip** pulses with eclectic characters and massive billboards. The area is also the heart of the gay and lesbian scene.

Between Los Angeles proper and the San Gabriel Mountains, **Pasadena** has long been a fashionable haunt. Its historic Old Town district (p. 54) is good for strolling.

> ### The Hollywood Sign
> Hollywood's, and indeed LA's, most recognisable landmark was built in 1923 as an advertising gimmick for a real estate development dubbed 'Hollywoodland.' Located on Mt Lee, in Griffith Park (2, B3), each letter is 50ft tall and made of sheet metal. It's illegal to hike up to the sign; for good views, head to Griffith Park Observatory or to the top of Beachwood Canyon Drive.

Santa Monica and **Venice** (p. 29) are buzzing tourist hubs by the beach, with teaming shops, bars and restaurants. More frolicking beach towns lie south of the airport: **Manhattan Beach's** downtown has chic boutiques and restaurants; **Hermosa Beach** is more funky and known for its nightlife; and **Redondo Beach** has a lovely harbour and pleasure pier.

Further south, the beaches of Orange County are the haunt of surfers, artists and retirees. **Seal Beach** has a pleasantly unrestored downtown, **Huntington Beach** is a surf mecca, **Newport Beach** has a huge pleasure-craft harbour, and **Laguna Beach** has secluded beaches, leafy streets and a host of art galleries.

Wealthy **Malibu** is a romantic destination and favourite of surfers and other sun lovers. For panoramic views, drive along the crest of the Santa Monica mountains on Mulholland Hwy.

El Capitan, one of LA's 'painted ladies'

MUSEUMS & GALLERIES

California Science Center
A hands-on, interactive, state-of-the-art facility with a 3-D IMAX cinema; it's a favourite family destination.
✉ USC campus, Exposition Park (2, D4) ☎ 323-724 3623 [e] www.casciencectr.org 🚌 DASH C to Exposition Park 🕘 10am-5pm $ free ♿ good

Getty Center
See page 20.

Huntington Library & Museum
The library's collection rivals that of the British Museum, with a Gutenberg Bible and a manuscript of Chaucer's *Canterbury Tales*. The art gallery, displaying mostly 18th century British and French paintings, ranks among the world's greatest.
✉ 1151 Oxford Rd, San Marino (1, H7) ☎ 626-405 2100 [e] www.huntington.org 🚌 MTA 79, 379 🕘 Tues-Fri 12-4.30pm, Sat, Sun & summer 10.30am-4.30pm $ $8.50 ♿ good; for info call ☎ 626-405 2100

LA County Museum of Art (4, E4)
One of the country's best art museums. The collection includes early Renaissance artists, plus the likes of Picasso, Kandinsky, Rothko and David Hockney. There's free jazz in the courtyard on Friday evenings.
✉ 5905 Wilshire Blvd, Beverly Hills ☎ 323-857 6000 [e] www.lacma.org 🚌 MTA 20, 21, 22, 217, 320 🕘 Mon, Tues & Thurs 12-8pm, Fri 12-9pm, Sat-Sun 11am-8pm $ $7 ♿ excellent

Museum of Contemporary Art
(3, F3) Designed by Japanese architect Arata Isozaki, MOCA houses a renowned collection of paintings, sculptures and photographs from the 1940s to the present.
✉ 250 S Grand Ave, Downtown ☎ 213-621 1749 [e] www.MOCA-LA.org 🚆 Pershing Square 🚗 parking in California Plaza Garage ($4) 🕘 Tues, Wed, Fri-Sun 11am-5pm, Thurs 11am-8pm $ $6; free Thurs 5-8pm ♿ excellent; for info call ☎ 213-621 1782

Museum of Tolerance (4, J3)
A gut-wrenching look at the oppression of blacks in America and the 20th century Holocaust in Europe.
✉ 9786 W Pico Blvd, Beverly Hills ☎ 310-553 9036 [e] www.wiesenthal.com 🚌 SM 7 🚗 free underground parking 🕘 tours leave continually Mon-Thurs 10am-4pm, Fri 10am-1pm, Sun 10.30-5pm $ $8 ♿ excellent

David Peevers

Contemporary reflections at MOCA

Norton Simon Museum
Asian sculpture and an outstanding collection of works by Botticelli, Cézanne, Degas, Matisse, Monet and more.
✉ 411 W Colorado Blvd, Pasadena (1, H7) ☎ 626-449 6840 [e] www.nortonsimon.org 🚌 MTA 180, 181, 402 🕘 Thurs-Sun 12-6pm $ $4 ♿ excellent

NOTABLE BUILDINGS

Biltmore Hotel
See page 19.

Bradbury Building
(3, F3) Designed in 1893 with help from a ouija board, and featured in the movie *Blade Runner*, the 5-storey galleried atrium with black filigree cast-iron banisters catches daylight streaming in through a glass roof.
✉ 304 S Broadway, Downtown ☎ 323-626 1893 🚌 DASH D 🕘 Mon-Fri 9am-6pm, Sat 9am-5pm $ free ♿ ground floor only

City Hall
See page 18.

Gamble House
Designed in 1908 by Green & Green, this is considered the world's best example of Craftsman-style bungalow architecture. Other G&G homes are on nearby Grand Ave and Arroyo Terrace, including Charles Green's former private residence at 368 Arroyo Terrace.
✉ 4 Westmoreland Pl, Pasadena (1, H7) ☎ 626-793 3334 [e] www.gamblehouse.usc.edu

🚌 MTA 180, 181 🕒 Thurs-Sun 12-3pm; 1hr tours every 20mins $ $5 ♿ ground floor only

Griffith Observatory & Planetarium (2, B4)
A local landmark set in Griffith Park, the observatory houses the hands-on Hall of Science astronomy museum, 2 telescopes and a planetarium with live multi-media presentations. The city view alone makes the trip worthwhile.
✉ **2800 E Observatory Rd, Griffith Park ☎ 323-664 1191 [e] WWW.griffithobs.org 🚌 MTA 96, 180, 181 🕒 park: 6am-10pm; Hall of Science: June-Sept 12.30-10pm; Oct-May 2-10pm (closed Mon); telescopes: 7-9.45pm (clear nights only); planetarium: call for show times $ planetarium $4/2-3 ♿ excellent**

Hollyhock House
Frank Lloyd Wright's earliest LA project (1921) extends interior living space outdoors and houses many original Wright-designed furnishings.
✉ **Barnsdall Art Park, cnr Hollywood Blvd & Vermont Ave, Hollywood (2, C4) ☎ 323-913 4157 [e] www.fohh.org 🚌 MTA 1 🕒 tours Wed-Sun at noon, 1, 2 & 3pm $ $2 ♿ excellent**

Hollywood Roosevelt Hotel (4, C2)
It hosted the first Academy Awards ceremony in 1929 and houses one of the best historical exhibits about Hollywood (mezzanine level).
✉ **7000 Hollywood Blvd, Hollywood ☎ 323-466 7000 🚌 MTA 1 $ free ♿ excellent**

LA Central Library (3, G2) This beaux-arts library is the 3rd-largest in America, with 2.1 million books and 500,000 historical photographs.
✉ **630 W 5th St, Downtown ☎ 213-228 7000 🚆 Metro Rail to Pershing Square 🚌 DASH B, C, E 🕒 Mon-Thurs 10am-8pm, Fri-Sat 10am-6pm, Sun 1-5pm $ free ♿ excellent**

Los Angeles Times Building
As you ascend through this 1935 Gordon Kaufman structure a tour guide explains the newspaper production process from A to Z.
✉ **202 S Spring St, Downtown (3, F3) ☎ 213-237 5757 🚌 DASH D 🅿 free parking at 213 S Spring St 🕒 tours Mon-Fri 11.15am $ free ♿ excellent; for info call ☎ 213-237 3178**

Mission San Juan Capistrano
One of California's most visited missions, with a lush garden and graceful arches. Legend has it that swallows return there every year on March 19th after wintering in South America; in fact they arrive over several weeks.
✉ **31882 Camino Capistrano, San Juan Capistrano (1, J7) ☎ 949-248 2048 🚆 Amtrak to/from LA or SD 🚌 OCTA 91 to Hwy 1, then No 1 north to Orange County beaches 🕒 8am-5pm $ $5/4 ♿ OK**

Schindler House
(4, F2) The unusual former home of Rudolph Schindler, a leading Modernist architect and disciple of Frank Lloyd Wright. It now functions as a think-tank for art and architecture but is open for touring.
✉ **835 N Kings Rd, Hollywood ☎ 323-651 1510 [e] www.mak.at 🚌 MTS 105 to Melrose Ave 🕒 Wed-Sun 11am-6pm $ $5 ♿ OK**

Union Station
See page 19.

Watts Towers (2, E4)
Under renovation but visible through the fence, Watts Towers is considered among the world's greatest works of folk art. Italian immigrant Simon Rodia used pipes,

Studio Tickets & Tours

Audiences Unlimited (☎ 818-506 0043) offers free tickets for *Mad About You, Friends, Home Improvement* and more. Tapings last 2-4hrs and are often booked out weeks in advance.

NBC Television (☎ 818-840 3537), 3000 W Alameda Ave, Burbank (2, B3), runs an informative studio tour ($7) on weekdays and summer weekends. Free tickets are available for live tapings of *The Tonight Show*.

Warner Brothers Studio (☎ 818-972 8687), 4000 Warner Blvd (2, B3), has 2hr 'VIP' tours of its sets and studios ($30). **Paramount** and **Universal** studios also offer tours; see page 36.

David Peevers
Mann's Chinese Theater

bed frames, steel rods and cement embellished with glass shards, tile, porcelain and seashells to build the structure from 1921-54.
✉ **1765 E 107th St, South Central LA ☎ 323-847 4646 ⏲ not recommended after dark**

FILM STUDIOS

Paramount Studios (4, B3) You're right in the middle of the studio hustle and bustle as a 2hr walking tour shows the real-life, workaday world of movie making. Call 5 days ahead for free tickets to TV shows.
✉ **5555 Melrose Ave, Hollywood ☎ 323-956 1777 [e] www.paramount.com 🚌 MTA 10 ⏲ Mon-Fri 9am-2pm $ $15 ♿ excellent**

Universal Studios (2, B3) The world's largest movie and TV studio, it also has a theme park with a Backlot Tour and rides re-creating such films as *Jaws*, *Jurassic Park* and *King Kong*. Universal Citywalk is a not-too-tacky shopping, dining and entertainment promenade.
✉ **100 Universal City Plaza, North Hollywood ☎ 818-508 9600 [e] www.universalstudios.com 🚌 MTA 420, 424, 425, 522; Airport Bus (☎ 800-772 5299) to/from Disneyland ⏲ June-Aug 8am-10pm; Sept-May 9am-7pm $ $38/28 ♿ excellent; for info ☎ 818-622 3801**

PARKS & WILDLIFE

Exposition Park (2, D4) What began as a farmers' market in 1872 now covers 160 acres and has 3 museums and the LA Memorial Coliseum. Across from the park is the **University of Southern California**; at the north-east corner of the campus is the Shrine Auditorium, home of the Grammy Awards and American Music Awards.
✉ **South Central LA 🚌 DASH C**

Long Beach Aquarium of the Pacific (2, H5) This is a 'must-see': sound effects, video, models and descriptive panels provide imaginative and educational information about more than 10,000 fish, mammals and birds.
✉ **310 Goldenshore St, Long Beach ☎ 526-590 3100 [e] www.aquariumofpacific.org 🚆 Metro Blue Line to Long Beach, then free Passport Shuttle ⏲ 10am-6pm $ $14.95/7.95-11.95 ♿ excellent**

LA's Painted Ladies

Some beautiful Art Deco theatres were built durin Hollywood's earliest growth spurt. At a time when th movies were considered vulgar, these eye-catchin theatres were dubbed 'painted ladies' because, like pro titutes, they lured folks to hand over their cash for a b of fun. Only some of the following places have bee restored to their former glory, but all are worth a loo

Egyptian Theater (1922), 6712 Hollywood Blvd (· C2) – inspired by the discovery of King Tut's tomb, is decorated with hieroglyphs and sphinx heads

El Capitan Theater (1926), 6838 Hollywood Blvd (· C2) – ornate Spanish Colonial façade and flambo ant East Indian-inspired interior

Los Angeles Theater (1931), 615 Broadway (3, G3) French baroque setting, vaulted ceilings, Corinthia columns and a lavish staircase leading to a crystal founta

Mann's Chinese Theater (1927), 6925 Hollywoo Blvd (4, C1) – ornate temple-like interior, but mo famous for its forecourt with hand-prints of the sta

Million Dollar Theater (1918), 307 Broadway (3, F3) notable for its squiggly, heavily ornamented façade

Orpheum Theater (1925), 630 Broadway (3, G3) French Renaissance-style building with a gold-le coffered ceiling and wrought-iron chandeliers

Wiltern Theater (1931), 3790 Wilshire Blvd (4, B5) Art Deco icon named for its location at the corner *Wil*shire and *Western* Blvds

SAN FRANCISCO & BAY AREA

Visually spectacular, historically colourful, and a regular trendsetter, San Francisco consistently tops the polls as America's favourite city. Compact, it covers the 7-by-7-mile tip of a 30-mile-long peninsula, with the Pacific Ocean to the west and San Francisco Bay to the east.

Downtown's long-time hub, **Union Square** is surrounded on all sides by boutiques and high-end hotels. There's ice skating in winter, street performers year-round. Extending from Union Square to Pier 1, the **Financial District** is rich in interesting architecture, including the Transamerica Pyramid, Russ Building, Pacific Coast Stock Exchange and Bank of America building (7, C4).

The tourist precinct of **Fisherman's Wharf** is home to an abundance of frivolous shops, silly museums and mediocre eateries. To its credit, it has a resident population of sea lions at Pier 39 (p. 64), historic ships moored at Hyde St Pier and an interesting maritime museum.

A once-legendary strip of brothels, opium dens and gambling dives, **Chinatown** is great for exploring. See page 53 for a walking tour.

The Castro is the gay centre; a great area for strolling, boutiquing, people-watching and getting your body pierced. The Castro Theater (p. 92) is the area's icon. Between here and Golden Gate Park, **The Haight** is famed as the former epicentre of the hippie movement. Today, the Upper Haight is lined with funky shops, cafes and cheap restaurants, while the Lower Haight is a scruffy few blocks of music clubs, cafes and dive bars.

Encompassing a large area south of **SoMa**, San Fran's rather dull version of SoHo, is the increasingly trendy **Mission District,** a Spanish-speaking enclave with a vibrant street life and cheap eats.

North Beach is the historic and vibrant Italian quarter, once the domain of the Beats, jazz bars and strip clubs. It's the place to hang-out late; for a game of bocci or a chat in Italian, head to Washington Square.

West of North Beach are the steep streets of **Russian Hill**, with some of the city's prime real estate as well as the crazily crooked 1000 block of Lombard St (7, D1). South from here are the exclusive old-school hotels atop **Nob Hill**; most structures survived the Big One of 1906.

Across the bay, **Berkeley** is the birthplace of the Free Speech movement and the California culinary revolution. It's also a mecca of liberalism and the bizarre, courtesy of the University of California, Berkeley (UCB).

Nearby **Oakland** has remarkable racial and economic diversity. Highlights include 1860s Victorian Row, vibrant Chinatown, the Art Deco Paramount Theater, Oakland Museum, Jack London Square on the waterfront and Lake Merritt.

Marin County is a great day-trip destination; see page 56 for a driving tour.

Old meets new: Transamerica Pyramid (1972) and Columbus Tower (1905)

MUSEUMS & GALLERIES
Ansel Adams Center
The works of Ansel Adams – best known for his B&W portraits of Yosemite National Park – illustrate the centre's raison d'être: promoting photography as an art.
✉ 250 4th St, SoMa (7, D5) ☎ 415-495 7000 @ www.friendsofphotography.org 🚇🚻 BART or Muni to Powell St 🚌 12, 14, 15, 30, 45 ⏰ 11am-5pm 💲 $5/3 ♿ excellent

Cable Car Barn & Powerhouse
Dating to 1910, the building's main function is as the power plant that tows all the system's cables – the mechanics of it all are quite an awesome sight. Exhibits include the original Clay St cable car and historic photographs and memorabilia.
✉ cnr Mason & Washington Sts, Nob Hill (7, D3) ☎ 415-474 1887 @ www.sfcablecar.com 🚻 Powell-Hyde, Powell-Mason cable cars ⏰ 10am-6pm 💲 free ♿ no

California Palace of the Legion of Honor
(6, K3) Built for the 1915 Panama-Pacific Exposition, this replica of the Palais de la Legion de Honneur (Paris), is one of San Francisco's premier art museums, with a world-class collection of medieval to 20th-century European art.
✉ Lincoln Park, Outer Richmond ☎ 415-863 3330 🚌 Muni 38 to 33rd Ave & Geary Blvd ⏰ Tues-Sun 9.30am-5pm 💲 $8/5 ♿ excellent; for info call ☎ 415-750 7645

Cartoon Art Museum
Not just fun and games, the exhibits show behind-the-scenes animation processes, the latest in animation technology and a wide range of still and animated cartoon works.
✉ 2nd fl, 814 Mission St, SoMa (7, D4) ☎ 415-227 8666 @ www.cartoonart.org 🚇🚻 BART or Muni to Powell St 🚌 Muni 9, 15, 30, 45; Golden Gate Transit 10, 20, 50, 60, 70, 80 ⏰ Wed-Fri 11am-5pm, Sat 10am-5pm, Sun 1-5pm 💲 $4 ♿ good

Exploratorium
See page 49.

Lawrence Hall of Science
See page 49.

Musée Mécanique
The world's largest private collection of 1920s self-playing musical instruments, mutoscope motion pictures and arcade games. It's in terrific working order, so bring lots of quarters.
✉ 1091 Point Lobos Ave, Outer Richmond (6, K3) ☎ 415-386 1170 🚌 Muni 18, 28, 38 ⏰ Mon-Fri 11am-7pm, Sat-Sun 10am-7pm 💲 free

Names Project Gallery
Recounts the ongoing creation and travels of the AIDS Memorial Quilt, The Castro's monument to the swathe AIDS has cut through the gay community. Each of the 25,000-plus individually crafted 6x3ft panels commemorates an AIDS victim.
✉ 2362a Market St, The Castro (7, H4) ☎ 415-863 1966 @ www.namesproject.org ⏰ 12-6pm 💲 free ♿ excellent

San Francisco Art Institute
Renowned for its Diego Rivera Gallery, with good examples of the Mexican artist's murals from 1931, the institute's courtyard and cloisters date to 1926. The cafe and views over the bay from its terraces are worth a trip in themselves.
✉ cnr Chestnut & Jones Sts, Russian Hill (7, C1) ☎ 415-771 7020 @ www.sfai.edu 🚇 BART to Montgomery St, then Muni 30 to Columbus Ave ⏰ Tues-Sat 10am-5pm 💲 free ♿ excellent

California Palace of the Legion of Honor, one of San Francisco's finest art museums

SFMOMA's modernist design sets the scene for its strong collection.

San Francisco Museum of Modern Art (7, D5)

SFMOMA's striking modernist design by Swiss architect Mario Botta is controversial, the permanent collection is strong in American abstract expressionism, and the photography collection is world class.

✉ 151 3rd St, SoMa ☎ 415-357 4000 🌐 www.sfmoma.org 🚇 BART Montgomery St 🚌 Muni 15, 30, 45; Golden Gate Transit 10, 20, 50, 60, 70, 80 ⏰ Fri-Tues 11am-6pm, Thurs 11am-9pm 💲 $8/4 ♿ excellent

Yerba Buena Center for the Arts

Not to be overlooked in a hasty rush to SFMOMA, the centre's galleries exhibit highly contemporary and insightful short-run shows.

✉ 3rd St, Yerba Buena Gardens, SoMa (7, D5) ☎ 415-978 2787 🌐 www.yerbabuenaarts.org 🚇 🚌 BART or Muni to Montgomery St ⏰ Tues-Sun 11am-6pm 💲 $5/3 ♿ excellent

NOTABLE BUILDINGS

Civic Center (7, F4)

Here stand the city's formal cultural and political units: the War Memorial Opera House (p. 91); the beaux-arts style City Hall, modelled after St Peter's Basilica in Rome; and the curved glass frontage of Louise M Davies Symphony Hall (p. 91).

☎ 415-864 3330 🚇 🚌 BART or Muni to Civic Center

Cliff House (6, K3)

Built in 1863 as an escape from the city's hectic pace, it has gone through myriad changes (documented in photographs that line the walls) and is now a good place for a sunset drink. The ruins in the cove just north are all that remain of **Sutro Baths**, a 6-pool, 3-acre indoor swimming palace built in 1886.

✉ 1091 Point Lobos Ave, Outer Richmond ☎ 415-386 3330 🚌 Muni 38 from Market St ⏰ 9.30am-10pm ♿ ground floor only

Coit Tower (7, C3)

Prime landmark built in 1934 and financed by San Francisco eccentric Lillie Hitchcock Coit who harboured a life-long passion for fire. Inside is a superb series of Diego Rivera-style murals painted by local artists in the 1930s.

✉ Pioneer Park, Telegraph Hill, North Beach ☎ 415-362 0808 🚌 Muni 15, 30, 32 ⏰ 10.30am-7.30pm 💲 $3 to ride to the top ♿ no

Grace Cathedral

Popular for its meditational labyrinths, it has a rose window from Chartres, bronze doors cast from Ghiberti's *Gates of Paradise* in Florence, and an altarpiece, *The Life of Christ*, designed by Keith Haring and dedicated to the AIDS Memorial Chapel Project. A good time to visit is during choral vespers, Sunday 3.30pm and Thursday 5.15pm.

✉ 1100 California St, Nob Hill (7, D3) ☎ 415-749 6310 🚌 Muni 1 to Taylor St 🚋 C Line cable car ⏰ Sun-Fri 7am-6pm, Sat 8am-6pm ♿ excellent

Stanford University

Begun on a horse-breeding farm in 1891, this is California's wealthiest university. The campus has a mix of Romanesque and Mission Revival buildings, a church with a mosaic-tiled façade and pipe organ, a museum-like visual arts centre (☎ 650-723 4177) and the Rodin Sculpture Garden.

✉ Palm Dr, Palo Alto (5, D4) ℹ info booth (☎ 650-723 2560; Mon-Fri 8am-5pm), Memorial Auditorium in front of Hoover Tower; free 1hr

Murals adorn the interior of the 210ft Coit Tower

tours 11am & 3.15pm [e] www.stanford.edu 🚆 CalTrain from SF 🚌 Sam Trans 7F, 16F; Santa Clara Transportation Agency (☎ 408-321 5555) 300 to/from San Jose $ all-day parking $6

BAY ISLANDS

Alcatraz (5, C3)

The rocky island in the middle of San Francisco Bay was the most infamous prison in the USA from 1933-63. Known as 'the Rock', it was escape-proof, and though several inmates got off the island, none were known to reach land alive.

ⓘ Park Rangers (☎ 415-705 1042) for info & tours [e] www.nps.gov/alcatraz ⛴ Blue & Gold Fleet (☎ 415-773 1188) from Pier 41; book well ahead (☎ 415-705 5555) 🕒 boats depart 9.30am-2.45pm $ $11 ♿ SEAT shuttles hourly

Angel Island State Park (5, C3)

Used throughout the years as a military base, immigration station, WWII Japanese internment camp and US Army missile site, the island has some interesting forts and bunkers. Most recently it's been the site of a native-plant restoration project and is now a great place for hiking, biking and camping.

ⓘ Park Headquarters (☎ 415-435 1915) at Ayala Cove; tours available [e] www.cal-parks.ca.gov/DISTRICTS/Marin ⛴ Blue & Gold Fleet (☎ 415-773 1188) from Pier 41 (daily May-Nov, Fri-Sun only Dec-April); Angel Island-Tiburon Ferry (☎ 415-435 2131) daily June-Aug, Sat-Sun only Sept-May 🛏 campsite reservations ☎ 800-444 7275 🍴 Cove Cafe, at Ayala Cove

Follow the arrows to Alcatraz

John Elk III

PARKS & GARDENS

Mt Tamalpais State Park (5, B2)

In addition to 360° views of ocean, bay and hills, 2571ft 'Mt Tam' has untold acres of hill and dale that are home to deer, fox and bobcat, over 200 miles of hiking and biking trails, and a stand of old-growth redwoods. **Muir Woods National Monument** at the park's southern end, has stunning vistas. There's a 7 mile trail from the mountain to **Mill Valley**, home of California's oldest mill (1835) and Marin's most rustic town.

ⓘ Pantoll Station (☎ 415-388 2070; 801 Panoramic Hwy) has detailed maps ($1) and info [e] www.mtia.net 🚌 Golden Gate Transit (☎ 415-923 2000) 63 from the Golden Gate Bridge toll plaza (weekends & holidays only) 🚗 11 miles north of SF via Hwy 101 & Panoramic Hwy 🍴🛏 Mountain Home Inn (☎ 415-381 9000), 810 Panoramic Hwy ♿ excellent

Tilden Regional Park (5, B3)

Berkeley's crown jewel, this 2079-acre park has more than 30 miles of trails (from paved paths to hilly scrambles), a carousel, miniature railroad, lake, botanical garden, 18-hole golf course, environmental education centre and the Brazil Building, constructed for the 1908 World's Fair.

✉ Berkeley Hills ⓘ East Bay Regional Park District (☎ 510-562 7275) 🚌 AC Transit 67 from Berkeley BART station

University Botanical Garden

Set in the hills above UCB, the garden has more than 13,000 species, one of the most varied plant collections in the USA.

✉ 200 Centennial Dr, UCB campus, Berkeley (5, B3) ☎ 510-642 3343 🚌 AC Transit 8, 65 from Berkeley BART station; Hill Service Shuttle from UCB campus 🕒 9am-4.45pm $ free ♿ OK

RELAXATION

Kabuki Hot Springs

Soak away aches in these Japanese-style communal baths with a hot soaking pool, invigorating cold plunge, sauna and steam room. Traditional Shiatsu massage available by appointment.

✉ Japan Center, cnr Geary Blvd & Fillmore St (7, F2) ☎ 415-922 6000 [e] www.kabuki.com 🚌 Muni 22, 38 🕒 women: Wed, Fri & Sun 10am-10pm; men: Mon, Tues, Thurs & Sat 10am-10pm $ $10-$15 ♿ no

SAN DIEGO

Conservative, comfortable, affluent San Diego is a great place to enjoy the laid-back California lifestyle. Smaller and far more accessible than LA, it has enough sights to keep you busy for a few days, but don't expect any bustling excitement.

The **Gaslamp Quarter**, once lined with saloons, gambling joints, bordellos and opium dens, is now a National Historic District where restored buildings (1870s to 1920s) house restaurants, bars, galleries and theatres.

San Diego's **Embarcadero**, built almost entirely on landfill, is well manicured and a nice place to stroll past ships and seafood restaurants.

Old Town is the site of the first civilian Spanish settlement in California – the Pueblo de San Diego. Since 1968 it's been a State Historic Park, a pedestrian precinct with shady trees, a large open plaza and a gaggle of shops and restaurants.

A cohesive community of 2nd and 3rd generation families populate **Little Italy**, which has restaurants, imported food stores and cool furniture and art stores that cater to the architects and designers who've recently moved in.

Hillcrest is the vibrant centre of San Diego's gay community, full of bars, restaurants, bookstores, record shops and movie theatres.

The swanky, status-conscious suburb of **La Jolla** (pronounced 'la-hoy-a') has upscale shopping, fine dining, a scenic seafront and historic architecture. Stunning 360° views can be had by following La Jolla Scenic Dr to the top of Mt Soledad.

The 3 miles between **Pacific Beach** and **Mission Beach** has end-to-end bodies, cafes, beach bars, surf rentals and impossible parking. **Ocean Beach** (or OB, as it's known) has a long fishing pier, beach volleyball, sunset barbecues and good surf. Its Newport Ave strip is stocked with bars, eateries and surfwear shops.

MUSEUMS

Junípero Serra Museum
The first Spanish settlement in California was established in 1769 on Presidio Hill, overlooking the valley of the San Diego River. The attractive site is now occupied by the museum, an imitation Spanish building with artefacts and pictures from the Mission and Rancho periods.
✉ Presidio Dr, Presidio Park, Old Town (8, F3) ☎ 619-297 3258 🚌 5, 6, 44 to Taylor St 🚊 Blue Line to Old Town 🕘 Tues-Sat 10am-4pm, Sun 12-4pm $ $3 ♿ limited access

Maritime Museum
(9, C1) The *Star of India*, built on the Isle of Man and launched in 1863, is the highlight of this museum which has 2 other restored sailing vessels.
✉ 1306 N Harbor Drive, Embarcadero ☎ 619-234 9153 🚊 County Center/Little Italy 🕘 9am-8pm $ $5 ♿ limited access

Goin' Down to TJ

As a Mexican city, Tijuana (or TJ) is neither typical nor attractive, but as border towns go, it is almost an archetype, with gaudy souvenir shops, noisy bars and sleazy backstreets. Though more respectable than it once was, it has never fully overcome the 'sin city' image it acquired during US Prohibition. It still attracts young Americans who can legally get drunk from age 18, but these days most people can feel comfortable in the main shopping streets, at least until sunset.

A trolley runs from Downtown San Diego to San Ysidro every 15mins, from where you walk over a pedestrian bridge and through a turnstile into Mexico.

Museum of Contemporary Art (9, D2) The downtown branch of the La Jolla-based institution, it has shown innovative painting and sculpture since the 1960s. ✉ **1001 Kettner Blvd, Downtown ☎ 619-234 1001 🚆 Santa Fe Depot 🕘 Tues-Sun 10.30am-5.30pm (Fri till 8pm) $ $3/2 ♿ excellent**

NOTABLE BUILDINGS

Mission San Diego de Alcalá (8, E5) Moved a few miles upriver in 1773, and rebuilt several times after Indian attack, earthquake and deterioration, it now has a small congregation, a visitor centre and a sleepy old Spanish ambience. ✉ **Mission Rd, just south of Friars Rd, and east of I-15 ☎ 619-281 8449 🚆 East Line to Mission 🕘 9am-5pm $ $2 ♿ excellent**

Salk Institute (8, B2) This biomedical research centre, founded in 1960 by polio prevention pioneer Jonas Salk, is a masterpiece of modern architecture. Designed by Louis Kahn in 1965, the classically proportioned travertine marble plaza and cubist, mirror-image laboratory frame a perfect view of the ocean. ✉ **10010 N Torrey Pines Rd, La Jolla ☎ 858-453 4100 [e] http://pingu.salk.edu 🚌 MTS 41, 301 🕘 guided tours Mon-Thurs 11am & noon (call in advance) $ free**

PARKS & WILDLIFE

Balboa Park
See page 14.

Whitewashed façade of Mission San Diego de Alcalá

Cabrillo National Monument (8, H2) At the southern tip of Point Loma, the monument marks where Portuguese explorer Juan Rodríguez Cabrillo landed briefly in 1542. There are stunning panoramas over the bay and the visitor centre has good exhibits on the native inhabitants and natural history. Also interesting are the 1854 lighthouse, the tidepools on the ocean side, and whale watching in winter. ✉ **Cabrillo Memorial Dr (Hwy 209) ☎ 619-557 5450 [e] www.nps.gov/cabr 🚌 6A, 26 🕘 9am-5.15pm $ $5/car, $2/pedestrian ♿ excellent**

San Diego Zoo (8, F4) Renowned San Diego Zoo has more than 800 species in a beautifully landscaped setting. Highlights include Tiger River (a re-created Asian rainforest environment) and Gorilla Tropics (an African rainforest). Allow a full day's exploring. ✉ **2920 Zoo Dr, Balboa Park ☎ 619-234 3153 [e] www.sandiegozoo.org ⓘ Skyfari Aerial Tram extends across the park; bus tours available 🚌 7 from Downtown 🕘 vary; call ahead $ $16/7 ♿ good; for info ☎ 619-231 1515, ext 4526**

Stephen Birch Aquarium-Museum A public education project of Scripps Institute of Oceanography, one of the world's largest marine research institutions, the aquarium has more than 30 tanks and top-notch marine life and science displays. ✉ **2300 Exhibition Way, La Jolla (8, C1) ☎ 858-534 3474 [e] www.aquarium.ucsd.edu 🚌 MTS 34 to Downwind Way; SIO Shuttle from Mandeville Hall (UCSD campus), Mon-Fri only 🕘 9am-5pm $ $8.50/7.50; parking $3 ♿ excellent**

Torrey Pines State Reserve (8, A1) This reserve preserves the last mainland stands of the Torrey pine (*Pinus torreyana*), a species adapted to sparse rainfall and sandy, stony soils. Hiking trails traverse wonderfully eroded sandstone gullies en route to the seashore. Views are superb. ✉ **west of N Torrey Pines Rd ☎ 619-755 2063 [e] www.torreypine.org 🚌 MTS 41, 301 🕘 9am-sunset $ free; parking $4**

AROUND CALIFORNIA

CALIFORNIA DESERTS

Anza-Borrego Desert State Park (1, J8)
Spectacular 600,000 acres of desert scenery, dotted with short walks and wildflowers (Feb-Apr). Borrego Springs is a good day-trip destination, as it's home to the park's excellent visitor centre. Easy-to-reach sights include Font's Point and Borrego Palm Canyon.
[i] visitor centre ☎ 760-767 5311; 767 4684 for wildflower update [e] http://cal-parks.ca/gov/DISTRICTS/colorado/abdsp622 🚗 2½hrs from SD via: I-8 to S-2; Hwy 78 through Julian; or Hwy 79 through Cuyamaca State Park 🕘 visitor centre: Oct-May 9am-5pm; June-Sept weekends only $ $5/day if you venture off the main hwys

Death Valley
See page 16.

Joshua Tree National Park (1, J8)
Small and popular desert park, known for its spiky Joshua trees, climber-friendly rock formations, short hikes and mountain-bike routes. Head to Keys View for sunset panoramas, Cholla Cactus Garden for sunrise.
[i] Oasis Visitors Center (☎ 760-367 7511; 8am-5pm), Twentynine Palms; emergency assistance ☎ 909-383 5651 [e] www.nps.gov/jotr 🚗 62 miles north of Palm Spring via Hwy 62 $ $10/car, $3/pedestrian (valid 7 days) 🍴 Jeremy's in Joshua Tree 🛏 J Tree Inn B&B (☎ 760-366 1188) & Mohave Rock Ranch (☎ 760-366 8455) in Joshua Tree

Palm Springs (1, J8)
The original and most visited of the so-called 'resort cities' in the Coachella Valley. A favourite with retirees and college kids, there's a growing gay scene. A ride on the aerial tramway is a must, as is visiting the nearby canyons and desert areas, including the Agua Caliente Indian Reservation and the San Jacinto Mountains. There's also some worthwhile museums.
[i] visitor centre (☎ 760-778 8418), 2781 N Palm Canyon Dr [e] http://palm-springs.org 🚌 Greyhound (☎ 760-325 2053) to/from LA; Amtrak to/from Oakland 🚗 3hrs east of LA via I-10; 3½hrs north-east of SD via I-15, I-215 & I-10 ✈ Palm Springs Regional Airport (☎ 760-323 8161); flights to/from LA & SF 🍴 see page 81 🛏 see page 105

CENTRAL COAST

Big Sur
See page 15.

Hearst Castle
See page 22.

Monterey Peninsula
See page 26.

Morro Bay (1, G4)
Morro Bay is both tourist trap and honest-to-goodness fishing town. The landmark 576ft Morro Rock was named by explorer Juan Cabrillo for the domed turban hats worn by the Moors of Spain. An old paddlewheeler does harbour tours with a Dixieland jazz band, there are fishing trips and an aquarium where sick seals and sea lions are nursed. **Montaña de Oro State Park**, 6 miles south, has massive sand dunes and is good for hiking and biking.
[i] Chamber of Commerce (☎ 805-772 4467), 880 Main St [e] www.morrobay.com 🚌 CCAT (☎ 805-541 2228) to/from SLO & San Simeon (Hearst Castle) 🍴 Dorn's; Whale's Tail Restaurant 🛏 Pleasant Inn Motel (☎ 805-772 8521), 235 Harbor St; Blue Sail Inn (☎ 805-772 7132), 851 Market Ave

San Luis Obispo (1, G5) SLO is large enough to support a major university, diverse nightlife and good restaurants and museums, yet small enough to inspire sobriquets like 'charming' and 'off the beaten path'. Its Spanish

SLO Farmers Market
Every Thursday night (6-9pm), a lively gathering of farmers' market stalls takes over Higuera St, San Luis Obispo, and turns it into a giant street party. Barbecues belch smoke, families stroll and street performers do their thing – it's one of California's best evening outdoors events.

mission is a historic beauty. ⓘ **SLO Chamber of Commerce** (☎ 805-781 2777), 1031 Chorro St 🌐 **www.SanLuisObispo County.com** 🚆 Amtrak to/from LA & Sacramento 🚌 Greyhound to/from LA & Sacramento; CCAT (☎ 805-541 2228) to Morro Bay & nearby beach towns ✈ American Eagle flights to/from LA & SF ✕ see page 82 🛏 see page 106

Santa Barbara (1, H5)
Marketing itself as the 'California Riviera', Santa Barbara has a seaside location, affluent population and Mediterranean architecture. Beyond the snobbish boutiques and eateries is a raucous student population, sizeable boating community, notable museums, a well-preserved Spanish mission and miles of beachfront bike trails. The Santa Barbara Trolley (☎ 805-965 0353) does a narrated 90-minute loop past points of interest; see page 55 for a walking tour. ⓘ **info centre** (☎ 805-965 3021; 9am-5pm), cnr Garden St & Cabrillo Blvd; **Hot Spots Visitor Centre** (☎ 805-564 1637; 9am-9pm), 36 State St 🌐 **www.santa barbaraca.com** 🚆 Amtrak to/from LA & SF 🚌 Greyhound to/from LA & SF 🚗 160 miles north of LA via Hwy 1 or 101 ✈ flights to/from LA ✕ see page 82 🛏 see page 106

Santa Cruz (5, F4)
A popular weekend escape from San Francisco that caters to health-conscious hippies – think herbal spas, massage and organic

eateries. Home to the University of California, Santa Cruz (UCSC) and its 10,000 students, the city is serene most of the year, except on summer weekends. The Boardwalk is the oldest beachfront amusement park on the West Coast; the 1923 Giant Dipper coaster and 1911 Looff carousel are both National Historic landmarks. ⓘ **Visitor Information Center** (☎ 831-425 1234; Mon-Sat 9am-5pm, Sun 10am-4pm), 701 Front St 🌐 **www.sc ccvc.org/about/sc; university: www.ucsc.edu** 🚌 Greyhound to/from SF & LA; buses to/from CalTrain/Amtrak station in San Jose; Santa Cruz Airporter (☎ 831-423 1214) to San Jose & SF airports ✕ Cafe Pergolesi; see also page 82 🛏 Carmelita Cottages Hostel (☎ 831-423 8304), 321 Main St; Pacific Inn (☎ 831-425 3722), 330 Ocean St

Santa Cruz's historic Boardwalk

GOLD COUNTRY
Columbia (1, E5)
The best preserved Gold

Country town, its central 4 blocks are a State Historic Park where 1850s buildings house history displays and concessionaires wear period costumes. The blacksmith and shoemaker use traditional methods, and a horse-drawn carriage is the only vehicle allowed on the streets. ✉ **5 miles north of Sonora** ⓘ **Columbia Museum** (☎ 209-532 4301), cnr Main & State Sts 🌐 http://cal-parks.ca /gov/DISTRICTS/calveras/ Columbia/cshp ⏰ museum & most shops: 10am-4.30pm (to 6pm May-Sept) 💲 free ✕ 🛏 City Hotel (☎ 209-532 1479)

Grass Valley & Nevada City (1, D4)
These neighbouring towns have historic districts, good restaurants, nightlife and shops. Surrounding them are blockbuster mines-turned-museums: Empire Mine State Historic Park (☎ 530-273 8522) sits atop 367 miles of mine shafts which operated from 1850-1956; the North Star Mining Museum (☎ 530-273 4255) has a Pelton water wheel collection and mining equipment. ⓘ **132 Main St, Nevada City** (☎ 530-265 2692) 🌐 **www.ncgold.com** 🚆 Amtrak to/from Sacramento; Gold Country Stage between the 2 towns (7.30am-6pm) 💲 Empire Mine: $3; North Star: by donation ♿ good ✕ see page 80 🛏 Kendall House (☎ 530-265 0405), 534 Spring St, Nevada City

Murphys (1, E5)
Quaint Murphys looks like a cross between a Norman Rockwell painting and a Jimmy Stewart western.

Attractions include better-than-average restaurants, wine tasting rooms (notably Kautz-Ironstone) and the Mercer Caverns (☎ 209-728 2101; $5), with its stalactites, stalagmites and vaulted chambers. Nearby **Caliveras Big Trees State Park** has giant sequoia trees.

🚌 **Stagecoach Limousine Service** (☎ 209-736 9226) to/from SF, San Jose & Oakland airports ⊘ caverns: Oct-May 10am-4pm (to 8pm Fri-Sat), June-Sept 9am-8pm ✕ **Murphy's Bagel Barn** ⇌ **Murphys Historic Hotel & Lodge** (☎ 209-728 3444)

Sutter Creek (1, E4)
Once California's main foundry centre, now one of the Gold Country's most endearing towns, with raised sidewalks and high-balconied buildings free of modern additions. Day-trip destinations abound: Chaw'se Indian Grinding Rock State Historic Park (☎ 209-296 7488; $5) contains Miwok petroglyphs and mortar holes; Daffodill Hill blooms March-April; and Steiner Rd has excellent wineries.

ⓘ **Bubble Gum Bookstore**, 59 Main St, for guidebooks & maps 🌐 www.amadorcounty. com ✕ see page 81 ⇌ **Sutter Creek Inn** (☎ 209-267 5606), 75 Main St

NORTH COAST
Bodega Bay (5, A1)
A small fishing town with beaches, tidepools, weekend whale-watching trips, diving and good surf, it was the setting for Alfred Hitchcock's 1963 film *The Birds*.

ⓘ **Chamber of Commerce** (☎ 707-875 3422; Mon-Fri 9am-5pm) 🌐 www.bodegabay.com 🚌 **MTA** (☎ 707-884 3723), between Point Arena & Santa Rosa 🚤 56 miles north of SF on Hwy 1 ✕ **Tides Wharf & Lucas Wharf** restaurants on Hwy 1 ⇌ **Bay Hill Mansion B&B** (☎ 707-875 3577), 3919 Bay Hill Rd

Eureka (1, B2)
Eureka, charmingly historic and provincial, is the largest town on California's northern coast. Humboldt Bay lodges a significant fishing fleet, and Old Town has historic Victorian homes, impressive museums and good restaurants. The bay cruise on the MV *Madaket* (☎ 707-445 1910) is popular, as is the Samoa Cookhouse (p. 80).

ⓘ **Visitors Bureau** (☎ 707-443 5097; Mon-Fri 9am-5pm) 🌐 www.eureka-touris m.com 🚌 Greyhound (☎ 707-442 0370; 1603 4th St) to/from Arcata, Healdsburg & SF; Amtrak Thruway connects with Amtrak trains at Martinez; Redwood Transit System (☎ 707-443 0826) to/from nearby towns ✈ Arcata-Eureka Airport (20 miles north); flights to/from LA & SF ✕ see page 80 ⇌ see page 104

Ferndale (1, B2)
An idyllic dairy farming community, Ferndale seems like time has passed it by. The town has ornate mansions known as 'butterfat palaces', because the original settlers grew wealthy from dairy farming. The

nearby **Lost Coast** area offers pristine coastline and a walking trail that passes old shipwrecks and an abundance of wildlife.

ⓘ *Victorian Village of Ferndale* map available at the Kinetic Sculpture Museum ✕ **Hotel Ivanhoe** (Italian); **Curley's Grill** ⇌ **Gingerbread Mansion** (☎ 707-786 4000), 400 Berding St

Guerneville (1, D3)
The biggest town on the Russian River, with hotels, restaurants and surrounding wineries, including Korbel Champagne Cellars' 1886 vineyard (☎ 707-869 2772; 13250 River Rd). Two miles north is Armstrong Redwoods State Reserve, with a magnificent stand of old-growth redwood forest.

ⓘ **Visitors Bureau** (☎ 707-869 9212), 14034 Armstrong Woods Rd 🌐 www.men.or./1/rrparks/ rrweb 🚌 **Sonoma County Transit 20** to/from Santa Rosa 🚤 60 miles north of SF off Hwy 116 ✕ **Hub Cap Cafe & Deli; Applewood Inn** (fine dining) ⇌ **Applewood Inn** (☎ 707-869 9093), 13555 Hwy 116

Mendocino (1, D2)
This photogenic town perched on a bluff overlooking the Pacific is noted for its Cape Cod-style architecture and active arts community. The whole town is on the National Register of Historic Places; outdoor activities, hot tubs and massage are also on offer.

ⓘ **Ford House Visitor Center & Museum** (☎ 707-937 5397; 11am-

4pm), 735 Main St **&** www.mendocinocoast.com; www.mendocino.org **⌕** Mendocino Stage (**☎** 707-964 0167) & MTA (**☎** 800-696 4682) in local area; change in Santa Rosa for Sonoma & SF **✕** see page 81 **⛴** see page 105

The Redwoods
See page 25.

Trees of Mystery
A giant redwood carving of Paul Bunyan and Babe the Blue Ox towers over the entrance to the Trees of Mystery walking trail which passes a number of unusual trees, redwood carvings and other nature-made oddities. The End of the Trail Museum has an outstanding collection of American Indian artefacts. ✉ Hwy 101, 5 miles north of Klamath (1, A2) **☎** 707-482 2251 **&** www.treesofmystery.net **⌕** Greyhound north & south ⏲ 8am-7pm (last entry 5.45pm) **$** $6.50/4 **✕** Klamath Inn (dinner only) **⛴** Klamath Inn (**☎** 707-482 1425), 451 Requa Rd, west of Hwy 101

NORTHERN MOUNTAINS
Lassen Volcanic National Park (1, B4)
Lassen Peak (10,457ft), which last erupted in 1915, is the world's largest plug-dome volcano. The park also has boiling hot springs, steaming sulphur vents and tube caves. ⓘ Park HQ (**☎** 530-595 4444), Hwy 36 near Mineral; Manzanita Lake Visitor Center (**☎** 530-595 4444, ext 5180) at north entrance

& www.nps.gov/lavo **⌕** 50 miles east of I-5 via Hwys 36 & 299; Hwy 89 provides access to geothermal areas, hiking trails & campgrounds **$** $10 (valid 7 days) **⛺** campgrounds & cabins available

Lava Beds National Monument (1, A4)
A remarkable volcanic park with lava flows, craters and dozens of lava tubes. The visitor centre provides free flashlights and helmets for self-guided exploring. ✉ 58 miles north-east of Mt Shasta, via Hwys 97 & 139 ⓘ visitor centre (**☎** 530-667 2282), south end of park **&** www.nps.gov/labe ⏲ May-Sept 8am-6pm, Oct-Apr 8am-5pm **$** $4/car, $2/bicycle or pedestrian **⛺** campground; motels in nearby Tulelake

Mt Shasta (1, B3)
Dwarfed by its namesake mountain, this scenic town makes an excellent base for hiking, mountain biking, climbing and skiing. Along with plenty of good places to stay and eat, there's a good museum and a fish hatchery.

ⓘ Visitors Bureau (**☎** 530-926 4865), 300 Pine St; Ranger District Office (**☎** 530-926 4511), 204 W Alma St **&** www.r5.fs.fed.us/shastatrinity **⌕** Greyhound north & south on I-5; STAGE (**☎** 530-842 8295) to/from surrounding areas **⌕** 60 miles north of Redding off I-5 **✕** Wendie's Italian Restaurant; Willy's Bavarian Kitchen **⛴** Mt Shasta Ranch B&B (**☎** 530-926 3870), 1008 WA Barr Rd; Mt Shasta Resort (**☎** 530-926 3030), 1000 Siskiyou Lake Blvd

SACRAMENTO (1, D4)
California State Capitol
Built in the late 1800s and carefully restored, its rooms on the ground floor contain furniture, photographs and documents from various periods. Assembly and Senate rooms are open to the public when parliament is in session. ✉ cnr 10th St & Capitol Mall **☎** 916-324 0333 **⌕** Downtown Area Shuttle ⏲ Mon-Fri 7am-6pm, Sat-Sun 8.30am-4pm; tours hourly 10am-4pm **$** free **♿** good

---

Spirit of Sacramento
The *Spirit of Sacramento*, an 1842 paddlewheeler does a 1hr narrated tour of the Sacramento River that's worth the $10 ticket. The boat leaves from the L St dock next to the visitor centre; for information call **☎** 916-552 2933 or 800-433 0263.

Lady in Purple
The decor in *Fat City*, one of Sacramento's best-known restaurants, is worth a look – the bar came from Leadville, Colorado, in 1876 and the stained-glass 'Lady Wearing Purple' won first prize at the 1893 Chicago World's Fair.

California State Railroad Museum
A world-class collection of locomotives, freight and passenger cars, toy models and memorabilia.
✉ cnr 2nd & I Sts ☎ 916-445 6645 [e] www.csrmf.org 🚌 DASH from downtown 🕘 10am-5pm $ $6 ♿ museum is excellent, trains poor

Old Sacramento
Once a bustling river port filled with hopeful gold seekers, 'Old Sac' contains California's largest concentration of buildings on the National Register of Historic Places. The buildings now house candy stores, T-shirt shops and restaurants.
[i] visitor centre (☎ 916-442 7644), 1101 2nd St [e] www.oldsacramento.com 🚌 DASH from downtown 🕘 visitor centre: 9am-5pm; most shops 9am-6/7pm

Sutter's Fort
Once the only trace of civilisation for hundreds of miles, the fort has been restored to its 1850s glory and has some fascinating artefacts. Self-guided audio tours available.
✉ cnr 27th & L Sts ☎ 916-445 4422 [e] http://cal-parks.ca/gov/DISTRICTS/goldrush/sfshp 🚌 DASH along J St 🕘 10am-5pm $ $3 ♿ OK

SIERRA NEVADA

Bishop (1, E6)
Major pit-stop for skiers and hikers. The old part of town has lots of character, with covered sidewalks, 1950s neon signs and hunting and fishing stores aplenty. The new parts have fast-food restaurants, chain motels and gas stations. Also worth a stop is Laws Railroad Museum (☎ 760-873 5950; $3), 4 miles north-east.
[i] visitor center (☎ 760-873 8405; Mon-Fri 9am-4.30pm, Sat-Sun 10am-4pm), 690 N Main St; White Mountain Ranger Station (☎ 760-873 2500), 798 N Main St [e] www.bishopvisitor.com; www.bishopweb.net 🚌 Greyhound to/from LA & Mammoth Lakes 🍴 Erick Schat's Bakkery; Whiskey Creek (fine food) 🛏 numerous along US 395 (Main St)

Kings Canyon & Sequoia National Parks
See page 23.

Lake Tahoe
See page 24.

Mammoth Lakes
(1, E6) The town of Mammoth Lakes is a service centre for Mammoth Mountain, a world-class skiing destination and mountain-bike park. The basalt towers of Devil's Postpile National Monument and the pristine lakes south and west of town are popular with hikers and backpackers.
[i] ranger station (☎ 760-924 5500) & visitor bureau (☎ 760-934 2712) share a building on Hwy 203 (8am-5pm); Mammoth Mountain (☎ 888-462 6668) [e] www.visitmammoth.com; www.nps.gov/depo 🚌 Greyhound to/from LA & Bishop; free shuttle buses (☎ 760-934 0687) to/from ski fields ✈ TW Express (☎ 800-221 2000) to/from SF & LA $ ski-lift $47 🍴 Grumpy's; Loony Bean Coffee Roasting Co. 🛏 see page 105

Mono Lake (1, E6)
This is North America's second-oldest lake, an Ice Age remnant formed more than 700,000 years ago. Mono's ancient tufa towers, formed when calcium-bearing freshwater bubbles up through the alkaline lake, appear like drip sand castles on and near the lakeshore. The most photogenic concentration of tufa is at the South Tufa Reserve ($2), on the lake's south rim. Other highlights are the Black Point Fissures and Panum Crater.
[i] visitor centre, (☎ 760-647 6595), US 395, Lee Vining; ranger staton & visitor centre (☎ 760-647 3044) north of Lee Vining [e] www.monolake.org 🍴 Bodie Mike's Pizza; Nicely's Restaurant 🛏 Tioga Lodge (☎ 760-647 6423) on US 395, 2½ miles north of Lee Vining

Yosemite National Park
See page 32.

Tom Downs

Ancient tufa formations, Mono Lake

CALIFORNIA FOR CHILDREN

With an abundance of theme parks and hands-on museums, and a climate that allows year-round outdoor activity, California is a great place to visit with children. Hiring a car is a must if you are travelling between cities; take breaks regularly and plan diversions for drives through the unstimulating congestion of larger urban areas.

School holidays are from early June to early September and around Christmas and Easter. Many restaurant and motel chains offer specials for kids under 12.

LOS ANGELES

California Science Center
See page 34.

Disneyland
See page 17.

Knott's Berry Farm
An Old West amusement park, with a *Peanuts* theme (remember Snoopy and Charlie Brown?), roller coasters, staged gun fights and gold-panning demonstrations. It's less crowded than Disneyland and plenty of fun.
✉ 8039 Beach Blvd, Buena Park, Orange County (1, J7) ☎ 714-220 5200 [e] www.knotts.com 🚆 Amtrak to Fullerton station, then bus No 99 🚌 MTA 460 from Downtown LA; Knott's Berry Farm Express (☎ 800-828 6699) to/from nearby hotels 🚗 ample parking ($7) 🕘 May-Sept 9am-midnight; Oct-Apr: Mon-Fri 10am-6pm, Sat 10am-10pm, Sun 10am-7pm $ $36/26; $16.95 after 4pm ♿ excellent; for info ☎ 714-220 5220

Lee Foster
Knott's Berry Farm fun

Long Beach Aquarium of the Pacific
See page 36.

LA Children's Museum (3, E4)
Plenty of fun, with hands-on displays and educational games.
✉ 310 N Main St, Downtown ☎ 213-687 8800 🚌 DASH D 🕘 May-Sept 10am-5pm, weekends rest of year $ $5 ♿ excellent

Six Flags Magic Mountain
Ten themed areas packed with rides, including the highest, fastest, wildest and most hair-raising roller coasters in California. **Hurricane Harbor** next door is a water park extraordinaire.
✉ Valencia (1, H6) ☎ 818-367 9565 [e] www.sixflags.com 🚆 Metro Rail to Santa Clarita, then bus No 30 🕘 May-Sept 10am-10pm; Oct-Apr 10am-8pm (Magic Mountain only) $ $36 ♿ good

Universal Studios
See page 36.

SACRAMENTO (1, D4)

Waterworld USA
Besides the wave pool, where you can surf mini breakers, there's a tangle of water-slides, bumper cars, mini golf courses and carnival games. In a place where summer temperatures frequently top 100°F (38°C), this isn't just for kids.
✉ Cal Expo exit off I-80 ☎ 924-924 3747 🕘 10.30am-6pm $ $15

SAN DIEGO

San Diego Children's Museum (9, E3)
Best for ages 4 to 8, with giant construction toys, craft activities, storytelling and music.
✉ 200 W Island Ave,

Babysitters

Large hotel/motel chai rarely provide babys ters, but family owne places and B&Bs w usually help you loca one. It's generally easi to find someone in sun mer, on weekends early on weeknight because high school st dents make up th majority of the babys ting force. The averag wage is $5/hr per child

Gaslamp Quarter ☎ 619-233 8792 🚌 MTS 1, 3, 4, 16, 25 🕒 Tues-Sun 10am-5pm $ $4 ♿ excellent

San Diego Wild Animal Park
Herds of giraffe, zebra, rhino and other animals roam the open valley floor of this 1800-acre, free-range animal park. Visitors take a 50-minute ride on an electric tram, with great views of the animals and an interesting commentary. There's also a petting zoo and numerous excellent animal shows.
✉ 15500 San Pasqual Valley Rd, Escondido (1, J8) ☎ 760-747 8702 [e] www.sandiegozoo.org/wap/visitor_info.html 🚗 from I-15, exit at Via Rancho Parkway and follow the signs 🕒 9am-4pm (to 6pm May-Sept) $ $20/13; parking $3 ♿ good; for info call ☎ 760-738 5067

San Diego Zoo
See page 42.

Sea World (8, E2)
Very commercial, but the killer whale and dolphin acts are entertaining, while the Shark Encounter and Hidden Reef are almost educational.
✉ Sea World Dr, Mission Bay ☎ 619-226 3901 [e] www.seaworld.com/seaworld/sw_california/swcframe.html 🚌 MTS 9 🕒 varies; call for times $ $39/30; parking $5 ♿ good

SAN FRANCISCO & BAY AREA

Bay Area Discovery Museum
Housed in converted military barracks, this hands-on museum (especially designed for children) includes an underwater sea tunnel, ceramic studio, media centre and science lab.
✉ Fort Baker, Marin Headlands (5, C2) ☎ 415-487 4398 [e] www.badm.org 🚗 from SF, cross Golden Gate Bridge & take Alexander exit off Hwy 101 🕒 Tues-Sun 10am-5pm $ $7/6 ♿ excellent

Exploratorium (6, F1)
Established in 1969 as a museum of art, science and human perception, it's enormously popular with kids. A highlight is the Tactile Dome, a pitch-black dome that you can crawl, climb and slide through (advance bookings required).
✉ cnr Lyon & Bay Sts, The Marina ☎ 415-561 0360 [e] www.exploratorium.org 🚌 Muni 22, 28, 30, 41, 43, 45 🕒 Tues-Sun 10am-5pm (to 9.30pm Wed) $ $9/5 ♿ OK

Lawrence Hall of Science
Named after Nobel Prize winner Ernest Lawrence, it has a huge collection of exhibits on subjects ranging from lasers to earthquakes. Outdoor displays, including a 60ft model of a DNA molecule, compete with the breathtaking bay view.
✉ Centennial Dr, near Grizzly Peak Blvd, Berkeley Hills (5, B3) ☎ 510-642 5132 [e] www.lhs.berkeley.edu 🚌 AC Transit 8, 65 from Berkeley BART station; Hill Service Shuttle from UCB 🕒 10am-5pm $ $6/4 ♿ excellent

Six Flags Marine World
With killer whale shows, elephant rides and a 3-D motion simulator that takes you to the heart of an active volcano, this place offers as much excitement as one should be exposed to in a day.
✉ 2001 Marine World Pkwy (off I-80), Vallejo (5, B3) ☎ 707-643 6722 [e] www.sixflags.com/marineworld ⛴ Blue & Gold Fleet to/from SF's Pier 39 🕒 10am-10pm (earlier in winter) $ $31/21; parking $6 ♿ good

SAN LUIS OBISPO (1, G5)

San Luis Obispo Children's Museum
This amusing place has hands-on activities and interactive displays that teeter between being educational and fun.
✉ 1010 Nipomo St ☎ 805-544 5437 🚌 SLO Transit 2, 6 🚋 SLO Trolley to Nipomo 🕒 Thurs-Tues 10am-5pm $ $4 ♿ excellent

La Brea (Tar) Pits

On Wilshire Blvd, between La Brea & Fairfax Avenues, is a pit of *brea* (tar in Spanish) where, in 1906, paleontologists found the skeletons of over 200 Pleistocene era mammals. Children love the hands-on **George C Page Museum** (☎ 232-936 2230) that explains the natural history of the now not-so-natural area.

KEEPING FIT

California is the only place in the USA where you can surf in the morning and ski in the afternoon. The activity du jour largely depends on the region and season – skiing is more popular in the Sierra, rock climbing is huge in Yosemite, roller-blading and golf are loved everywhere.

Golf

California's concentration of courses is ironically greatest where there is the least water: Palm Springs, Palm Desert and San Diego. Also good are San Luis Obispo County and Monterey/Salinas. Green fees are high and tee times should be booked a week in advance.

Hiking & Backpacking

Hiking in national parks can be crowded, but the well-maintained trails are good for people with little experience and/or limited time. Hikers seeking true solitude should try national forests, especially wilderness areas. Most national parks require overnight hikers to carry backcountry permits, available from visitors centres or ranger stations.

Mountain Biking

Mt Tamalpais, Marin County, claims to be the birthplace of mountain biking. California's current mecca, however, is Mammoth Mountain. Lake Tahoe's Squaw Valley USA and Marlette Flume Trail, as well as the Central Coast's Montana de Oro State Park, are other hot spots.

Rock Climbing & Mountaineering

El Capitan and Half Dome in Yosemite National Park are both legendary

Taking the plunge, Yosemite NP

big-wall climbs, while Joshua Tree National Monument is a mecca for those who value technique and finesse over magnitude. Mt Shasta, Lassen Peak and Mt Ritter (all above 13,000ft) are impressive mountaineering destinations, as is Mt Whitney (14,497ft).

Rollerblading

The prime venues for rollerblading are San Francisco's Golden Gate Park, LA's South Bay Trail and Ocean Front Walk (Venice), and San Diego's Mission Bay Park. Rental shops are plentiful in these areas. Beginners should wear a helmet and wrist, knee and elbow pads.

Neil Wilson

Diving & Snorkelling

La Jolla, Monterey and Santa Catalina Island have fantastic kelp beds which house a rich marine environment; reefs and a 200ft deep underwater canyon make La Jolla especially attractive for scuba diving. If you don't have the time, money or desire to dive deep, rent a snorkel, mask and fins. Gear is easily hired along the state's beaches.

Skiing & Snowboarding

The Sierra Nevada, Lake Tahoe and Mammoth Lakes are home to California's most popular downhill slopes. Along with big-name places like Squaw Valley USA, are small operations like June Mountain (near Mammoth Lakes), Bear Mountain (near Yosemite) and Boreal (at Lake Tahoe). Another pocket of ski slopes is in the San Bernadino Forest around Big Bear (east of LA). Lift tickets are around $45/day, and ski areas are often well equipped with places to stay, eat, shop and have fun. Child-care is usually available.

Surfing

Surfing is California's signature sport and you'll find surfboard rental stands on just about every beach from San Diego to Santa Barbara. The 'big three' surf spots are Rincon, Malibu and Trestles, all of them point breaks. San Onofre and San Diego's Tourmaline are good beginner spots. Surfboards can be hired for around $10/hr.

Surfing off Manhattan Beach, LA

Swimming

Beach swimming is best done in Southern California (south of Santa Barbara), where waters are warmest. In LA, the beaches of Santa Monica and, especially, South Bay offer terrific swimming, while in San Diego, La Jolla Cove, Mission Beach and La Jolla Shores are all good.

Some of Northern California's best swimming is in rivers and lakes – the Russian and Eel rivers have mellow currents, Lake Tahoe is cool but heavenly and Berkeley's Lake Anza has a guarded swim area and warmish water. Ocean and Stinson beaches (Marin) are the best places to swim near San Francisco.

Public pools usually charge a fee and the larger ones often have lap swimming hours; contact the local Department of Parks and Recreation for a list of local pools. High schools (June-Sept), colleges and universities are also good places to enquire.

Yoga

All styles of yoga are popular, some fitness-oriented, others focused on meditative stretching. Health food stores and alternative book stores are the best sources of information on classes. *New Times* (www.newtimes.com) is a weekly paper that has yoga and meditation listings. Classes usually cost around $10.

out & about

WALKING TOURS
Historic Hollywood

Start at the corner of Hollywood Blvd and La Brea Ave, where the Hollywood Walk of Fame **(1)** begins. Seek out the marble-and-bronze stars of your favourite entertainers as you stroll to the Hollywood Entertainment Museum **(2)**, with its state-of-the-art displays. Next up is the 1927 Hollywood Roosevelt Hotel **(3)**, which has a great historical exhibit and impressive lobby. Mann's Chinese Theater **(4)** and El Capitan Theater **(5)** are well-preserved old movie palaces which still show first-run films. A couple of blocks further, the Egyptian Theater **(6)** is Hollywood's oldest, built in 1922. On the next block is the area's oldest restaurant, *Musso & Frank Grill* **(7)**, a nostalgic place to stop for a snack. At Frederick's of Hollywood Lingerie Museum **(8)** you'll find Madonna's tasselled bustier and Robert Redford's boxer shorts. Two more serious galleries follow – Los Angeles Contemporary Exhibitions **(9)** and the LA Center for Photographic Studies **(10)**. Continue down Hollywood Blvd just over the Vine St intersection to see the incredible Pantages Theater **(11)**, then backtrack and turn right up Vine for The Palace **(12)**, a 1924 Art Deco building, and Capitol Records Tower **(13)**, designed to look like a stack of records.

SIGHTS & HIGHLIGHTS

Hollywood Walk of Fame
Hollywood Entertainment Museum
Hollywood Roosevelt Hotel (p. 35)
Mann's Chinese Theater (p. 36)
El Capitan Theater (p. 36)
Egyptian Theater (p. 36)
Musso & Frank Grill
Frederick's of Hollywood Lingerie Museum
Los Angeles Contemporary Exhibitions
LA Center for Photographic Studies
Pantages Theater
The Palace
Capitol Records Tower

---

distance 1½ miles **duration** 2hrs
start 🚌 MTA 1
end 🚌 MTA 1

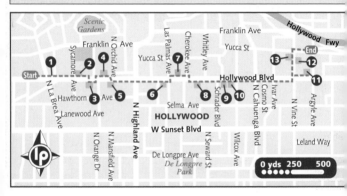

San Francisco's Chinatown

Start at the dragon-studded Chinatown Gate **(1)** and stroll past the shops and restaurants of Grant Ave to the Taoist Ching Chung Temple **(2)**. At the California St corner is Old St Mary's Church **(3)**, a 1854 Roman Catholic cathedral with a 90ft tower. Continue down Grant Ave, turn left at Sacramento St, pass the Chinese playground, then turn right at Stockton St, where there's exotic produce galore. Check out the historic Chinese Consolidated Benevolent Building **(4)** and Kong Chow Temple **(5)**, above the post office at No 855. Turn right into Clay St then left into colourful Waverly Place, with its 3 upstairs temples – Norras Temple **(6)** at No 109; Tin How Temple **(7)** at No 125; and Jeng Sen Temple **(8)** at No 150. Turn right into Washington St and stop for a bite at *Sam Wo's*, a hole-in-the-wall Chinese restaurant known for its gruff waiters.

Pass by the Bank of Canton **(9)** and Portsmouth Square **(10)**, where there's almost always a crowd playing checkers, chess, or mah-jongg. A pedestrian bridge crosses Kearny St to the Chinese Culture Center **(11)**, based at the Holiday Inn. Its changing Chinese art and culture exhibits are free. Head down Kearny St and turn left onto Commercial St to see the exhibits at the Chinese Historical Society Museum **(12)** and the Pacific Heritage Museum **(13)**. Return to Kearny St, continue south to California St and turn right, heading across St Mary's Square **(14)** to check out the serene-looking Sun Yat-sen statue.

distance 1 mile **duration** 2½hrs
start 🚋 Powell St cable cars
end 🚋 California St cable car

Vibrant Grant Avenue, hub of San Francisco's Chinese community

Old Town Pasadena

From Gamble House **(1)** on Orange Grove Blvd, walk south to Walnut St, where the Pasadena Historical Museum **(2)** occupies the Beaux Art-style Fenyes Mansion. Continue south down Orange Grove Blvd, under the Ventura (134) Fwy, and turn left on Colorado Blvd to reach the world-renowned Norton Simon Museum **(3)**. A little less than a mile east, Colorado Blvd meets Fair Oaks Ave, the heart of Old Town Pasadena, with restaurants, boutiques and antique shops in well-preserved vintage buildings. Grab lunch at the *Rack Shack* or the *Old Town Bakery*. Continue on Colorado Blvd, then head left on Los Robles Ave, where an Imperial Chinese façade marks the Pacific-Asia Museum **(4)**. Turn left on Union St, then right on Euclid Ave to reach the lovely fountains and pedestrian zone of the 1927 Pasadena City Hall **(5)** and the Plaza Las Fuentes **(6)**. Turn left into Walnut St, pass the Renaissance-style Pasadena Public Library **(7)**, then turn left again at Raymond Ave to pass Memorial Park. Continue on to Distant Lands travel bookstore **(8)** at No 56, then take a well-earned break in Central Park.

SIGHTS & HIGHLIGHTS

Gamble House (p. 34)
Pasadena Historical Museum
Norton Simon Museum (p. 34)
Pasadena City Hall
Pacific-Asia Museum
Plaza Las Fuentes
Pasadena Public Library
Distant Lands bookstore
Central Park

Fenyes Mansion (1905) is furnished with original period pieces.

David Peevers

distance 4 miles **duration** 3-4hrs
start 🚌 MTA 180, 181
end 🚌 MTA 180, 181 (from Orange Grove Blvd)

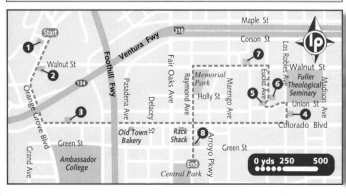

Santa Barbara Stroll

From the Museum of Natural History **(1)**, walk south on Mission Canyon Rd to the Mission Santa Barbara **(2)**. Turn left onto Laguna St, then veer right onto Mission St until you reach Santa Barbara St. Here there are lovely homes and the Alice Keck Park & Memorial Garden **(3)**. Turn right on E Micheltorena St and left on Anacapa St, which disects the lush and peaceful Alameda Plaza **(4)**. At E Sola St, turn right and then left on State St, passing the historic Arlington and Granada theaters before reaching the Santa Barbara Museum of Art **(5)**. Diagonally across the street, *Carlitos Cafe Y Cantina* **(6)** is good for lunch. Take E Anapamu St east to Anacapa St and turn right to reach the 1929, Spanish-Moorish revival Santa Barbara County Courthouse **(7)**, with its hand-painted ceilings and tiles from Tunisia and Spain. Continue south on Anacapa St and go left on E Canon Perdido St to El Presidio de Santa Barbara State Historic Park **(8)**, one of 4 remaining Spanish forts in California. From here turn right on Garden St and right again on E De La Guerra St, where an adobe complex houses the Santa Barbara Historical Museum **(9)** and its carved coffer that belonged to missionary Padre Junípero Serra.

distance 1½-2 miles **duration** 3-4hrs
start Santa Barbara Trolley
end State St Shuttle

Pegasus and his rotunda at the Museum of Natural History

David Peevers

DRIVING TOUR
Marin Headlands

From San Francisco, cross the Golden Gate Bridge, exit at Alexander Ave and dip left under the highway to scenic Conzelman Rd. First up is Battery Spencer **(1)**, dating to the Spanish-American War. The site includes a short trail that leads to a towering view of the Golden Gate Bridge. Continue up Conzelman Rd to Hawk Hill **(2)**, where thousands of migrating birds of prey soar along the cliffs from late summer to early autumn. There are several hiking trails in this area. Heading west, the road becomes a one-lane steep descent hanging above Bonita Cove. When the road forks, head left to Battery Mendell **(3)** and yet another sparkling view of San Francisco. Point Bonita Lighthouse **(4)**, built in 1877, is accessible by a breathtaking half-mile walking trail from here. The loop road continues around to Rodeo Lagoon and the Marin Headlands Visitors Center **(5)** on Bunker Rd. On the hill above the lagoon is the Marine Mammal Center **(6)**, which rehabilitates sea mammals before releasing them to the wild. Continue to the end of Bunker Rd and *picnic* at Rodeo Beach **(7)**, protected from wind by high cliffs. On your way back along Bunker Rd take the left-hand Field Rd fork and follow the signs to the Headlands Center for the Arts **(8)**, a refurbished barrack used as artist studios. Take Bunker Rd east back to Hwy 1; head north for Sausalito, south for San Francisco.

SIGHTS & HIGHLIGHTS

Battery Spencer
Hawk Hill
Battery Mendell
Point Bonita Lighthouse
Marine Mammal Center
Rodeo Beach
Headlands Center for the Arts

---

distance 12 miles **duration** 3-4hrs
start Golden Gate Bridge
end Hwy 1 (US101)

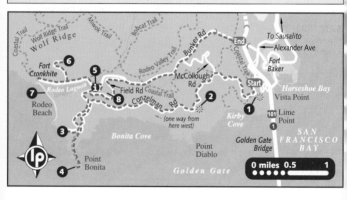

ORGANISED TOURS

LOS ANGELES

Casablanca Tours

One of the first tour guide companies in LA, they do specialised tours of the glamour and scandal of Hollywood, in mini-vans or tour buses.
✉ **Hollywood Roosevelt Hotel, 7000 Hollywood Blvd (4, C2) ☎ 323-461 0156 $ $41-45/26-28**

LA Conservancy

Offers an extensive program of walking tours that includes classic architecture, the Broadway movie palaces and historic homes.
✉ **727 7th St, Downtown (3, H2) ☎ 213-623 2489 $ $8**

)o-it-yourself

an Francisco lays out a ch feast for those keen n doing their sightsee-ıg on foot. The visitor ıformation centre has xcellent walking tour ·aflets to Chinatown, sherman's Wharf, North each, Pacific Heights nd Union Square.

SAN FRANCISCO

Chinese Culture Center

Choose from the Chinese Heritage Walk, which takes in architectural and historical points of interest, or the Chinese Culinary Walk, which focuses on cooking and buying food and includes a dim sum lunch.
✉ **Holiday Inn, 750 Kearny St, Chinatown (7, C3) ☎ 415-986 1822 [e] www.c-c-c.org $ Heritage Walk $15/6, Culinary Walk $30/15 🕐 Heritage: Sat 2pm; Culinary: Sat 10.30am**

Richard I'Anson

The Chinese first came to San Francisco during the 1849 goldrush.

Cruisin' the Castro

This 4hr walking tour gives the inside line on the history and culture of San Francisco's gay mecca. By reservation only.
✉ **375 Lexington Street, The Castro (mail only) ☎ 415-550 8110 [e] www.webcastro.com/castrotour $ $40; includes brunch 🕐 Tues-Sat 10am-2pm**

Dashiell Hammett Tour

One of San Francisco's best-known walks – up and down the streets of the Tenderloin and Union Square – led by author Don Herron. A book of the tour is available at City Lights (p. 66).
☎ 510-287 9540 $ $10 🕐 Sat 12-4pm (May & June only)

Haight-Ashbury Flower Power Walking Tour

See the site of the Human Be-In, the Drugstore Cafe, and the Grateful Dead's house on this 2hr tour; book ahead.
☎ 415-221 8442 $ $15 🕐 Tues & Sat 9.30am

SAN DIEGO

Gaslamp Quarter Historical Foundation

Ninety-minute guided walking tour offering a full historical picture of San Diego's historic Gaslamp Quarter.
✉ **William Heath Davis House (9, E4) ☎ 619-233 4692 [e] www.gqhf.com $ $5/3, children free 🕐 Sat 11am**

Gray Line

Narrated 4hr city tours twice daily, and extended itineraries to Tijuana, Ensenada, Wild Animal Park, Disneyland, Universal Studios and more.
✉ **Suite 130, 1775 Hancock St (8, F3) ☎ 619-491 0011 [e] www.graylinesandiego.com $ $25-58/11-41**

Old Town Trolley Tours

Loop around San Diego's main attractions in a streetcar, while listening to humorous commentaries from the conductor. Get on or off at any stop from 9am-6pm (to 10pm in summer).
✉ **2115 Kurtz St, Old Town (8, F3) ☎ 619-298 8687 [e] www.historictours.com $ $24/12**

AROUND CALIFORNIA

Santa Catalina Island Company
Forty-minute tours of the island's undersea gardens in a 60ft 'semi-sub' and 4hr inland motor tours exploring the island's rich landscape. A glass-bottom boat leaves several times a day from Avalon pier.
✉ cnr Caralina & Crescent Avenues, Avalon ☎ 310-510 2500 [e] www.catalina.com/scico $ $24.50 undersea gardens, $34.50 inland, $9 glass-bottom boat

Jeep Eco-Tours
Off-road journeys on Santa Catalina Island's back roads, accompanied by a botanist or a wildlife naturalist (your choice).
✉ PO Box 2739, Avalon CA 90704 ☎ 310-510 1421 $ $65 (2hrs); ½-day charter $495, full day charter $795 (up to 6 people)

Gray Line
Gray Line (☎ 415-558 400) runs daily tours to th **Wine Country**, visiting 3 wineries in Sonoma or Nap with complimentary wine tasting and a stop to sho and lunch on your own. Their **Marin County** tou includes visits to Sausalito and Muir Woods. Bot tours leave from the Transbay Terminal (6, D9), Sa Francisco, and require bookings.

Desert Adventures
Guided jeep tours to the Indian Canyons, Santa Rosa Mountains, around Bighorn Sheep Preserve, and other difficult-to-get-to areas. The driver/guides are informed about the natural environment and Indian lore; Sept-June only.
✉ Suite 555, 67 E Palm Canyon Drive, Cathedral City ☎ 760-324 JEEP, 888-440 5337 [e] www.red-jeep.com $ from $69 for 2hrs

Green Tortoise
Round-trip bus tours departing San Francisco for the Redwoods, Yosemite and the eastern Sierra Nevada.
✉ 494 Broadway, San Francisco (7, C3) ☎ 415-956 7500, 800-867 8647 [e] www.greentortoise.com $ varies

Valley Floor Tour
Two-hour tour in an open-air tram, which stops at points of interest including Yosemite Falls, Bridalveil Falls and El Capitan; the moonlight tour (summer only) is spectacular.
✉ Yosemite Valley, Yosemite National Park (1, E5) ☎ 209-252 4848 [e] www.nps.gov/yose $ $17

Seaview
For views of the kelp forests and schools of fish in Morro Bay, take a spin on this semi-sub which plies the waters daily.
✉ Marina Sq, 699 Embarcadero, Morro Bay (1, G4) ☎ 805-772 9463 $ $12.50/5.50

Richard I'Anson

Bridalveil Falls, Yosemite National Park

shopping

The sheer variety and quantity of consumer goods in the USA – and in California in particular – staggers many visitors. You can buy virtually anything you desire and lots more, for a price that is usually lower than just about anywhere else.

Apart from department stores, shopping malls, factory outlets, thrift stores and massive supermarkets, California has many shops which stock highly specialised goods.

The state's diverse communities provide a vast array of interesting products, from traditional Mexican crafts such as leather shoes, belts and embroidered fabrics to Guatemalan jackets and Indian incense. The Chinatown districts of San Francisco, Oakland and LA are full of Oriental wonders, from silk robes to dried sea creatures, plus a wonderful assortment of teas.

Basic California sales tax is 7.75%. For most purchases, a local (city or county) tax is added to this, which means you'll pay a different tax rate in every town.

Visa and MasterCard are accepted nearly everywhere, from gas stations to retail stores, hotels and restaurants (even tiny ones!). The least accepted card in California is American Express. It's generally OK to pay with travellers cheques, though in small, rural towns shops prefer credit cards or cash. ATMs are everywhere, including grocery stores, gas stations and convenience stores.

Opening Hours

Most independent retail stores are open from 9 or 10am to 5 or 6pm, with extended hours (8 or 9pm close) 1 day a week. On Sunday hours are shorter (usually noon-6pm) and on Monday shops are often closed. Department and chain stores tend to open daily, usually until 9pm Sunday to Thursday, and even later on Friday and Saturday. From late November until Christmas many large stores and shopping malls stay open till midnight.

In areas like LA's Melrose Ave and Old Town Pasadena, The Castro and Fisherman's Wharf in San Francisco and San Diego's Gaslamp Quarter and Hillcrest district, shops keep longer hours to meet customer demand.

David Peevers

Rodeo Drive – the epicentre of Beverly Hills swank and style.

LOS ANGELES

Melrose Ave (4, D3) has long been LA's epicentre of cool and *the* place for eccentric fashions. While mainstream icons like The Gap have moved in, the stretch between La Brea and Fairfax Avenues still has unique boutiques selling clothes, shoes and music.

In the **Design District** (4, G2), framed by Santa Monica, Beverly and La Cienega Blvds, hundreds of interesting shops, showrooms and art galleries emanate from the Pacific Design Center. Serious bargain hounds should head to the **Garment District** (3, J4) and **Jewelry District** (3, G3), a paradise of wholesale items in historic Downtown.

For cheap sunglasses, silly T-shirts, pop culture posters and brightly coloured garments (often African or Balinese), take a stroll along **Ocean Front Walk** (2, E1) in Venice Beach. Nearby are cool boutiques, cigar stores and myriad cafes along Santa Monica's **Main St** (2, D1). For ethnic souvenirs, head for **Olvera St** (3, D4) in El Pueblo de Los Angeles, **Chinatown** (3, C3), and the **Japanese Village Plaza** (3, E5).

Known the world over for its up-up-upscale designer boutiques and jewellery stores, antique shops, and high-priced salons, **Rodeo Drive** (4, H2) provides a tangible definition of Beverly Hills.

SHOPPING MALLS
Beverly Center (4, F2)
At the heart of West Hollywood, this multi-level mall is a boon to those who are born to shop. There are around 200 stores and 13 cinemas.
✉ 8500 Beverly Blvd, W Hollywood ☎ 310-854 0070 🚌 MTA 14, 16, 105, 202 ⊙ Mon-Fri 10am-9pm, Sat 10am-8pm, Sun 11am-6pm

Century City Center
David Peevers

Century City Center
(4, K3) The perfect California shopping mall, Century City is outdoors, has small boutiques, high-end chains, terrific kitchenware stores, a food court with Indian, Greek and Mexican food, and a huge movie complex.
✉ 10250 Santa Monica Blvd, Century City ☎ 310-277 3898 🚌 MTA 4, 22, 322 ⊙ Mon-Fri 10am-9pm, Sat 10am-6pm, Sun 11am-6pm

Santa Monica Place
In a Frank Gehry-designed structure near the Third St Promenade, the stores run the gamut from homewares to music and bath products.
✉ cnr Colorado Ave & Third St Promenade, Santa Monica (2, D1) ☎ 310-394 5451 🚌 MTA 20, 22, 33; SM 1, 2, 8, 9 ⊙ Mon-Sat 10am-9pm, Sun 11am-6pm

South Coast Plaza
An enormous complex of chain department stores (Macy's, Nordstrom, etc) and smaller boutiques, this place is an Orange County consumer landmark. Don't miss the sculpture garden by Isamu Noguchi.
✉ 3333 Bristol St, Costa Mesa (1, J7) ☎ 714-435 2034 🚗 San Diego (405) Fwy to the South Coast Dr exit, then turn right ⊙ Mon-Fri 10am-9pm, Sat 10am-7pm, Sun 11am-6.30pm

Westside Pavilion
Westside's attractions are its affordable clothing shops, expensive boutiques and specialty shops, a 1950s carousel and a cinema that shows independent films.
✉ 10800 Pico Blvd at Westwood, West LA (2, D2) ☎ 310-474 6255 🚌 SM 7, 8, 12, 13 ⊙

Mon-Fri 10am-9pm, Sat 10am-8pm, Sun 1-6pm

DEPARTMENT STORES

Barneys (4, H2)

The relatively new kid on the block, Barneys has a terrific rooftop deli with views of the Hollywood Hills, plus all the designer clothes, make-up and jewellery you could need.

✉ 9570 Wilshire Blvd, Beverly Hills ☎ 310-276 4400 🚍 MTA 20, 21, 22 ⊕ Mon-Fri 10am-6pm (Thurs till 7pm), Sat-Sun 12-6pm

Neiman Marcus

(4, J2) Besides clothes, jewellery, shoes and handbags, 'Neimans' does a great line of sweets and other edible treats.

✉ 9700 Wilshire Blvd, Beverly Hills ☎ 310-550 5900 🚍 MTA 20, 22, 27 ⊕ Mon-Fri 10am-6pm, Sat 10am-7pm, Sun 12-6pm

Saks Fifth Avenue

(4, H2) Everything from designer frocks to men's socks, under one roof that's been central to the Beverly Hills shopping scene since the 1920s.

✉ 9600 Wilshire Blvd, Beverly Hills ☎ 310-275 4211 🚍 MTA 20, 22, 27 ⊕ Mon-Sat 10am-6pm (Thurs to 8.30pm), Sun 12-6pm

MARKETS

Farmers Market

(4, E3) The city's best-known market, Farmers has 150 shops and stalls selling produce, gourmet food, unique crafts and gifts.

✉ 6333 W 3rd St, Fairfax District ☎ 323-933 9211 🚍 MTA 16,

Cooking up gumbo at the Farmers Market

217 ⊕ Mon-Sat 9am-7pm, Sun 10am-6pm

Grand Central Market

See page 63.

Wholesale Flower Market (3, H4)

One of the most colourful destinations in the city, the flower market offers the best selection of fresh blooms in the early morning.

✉ 754 S Wall St, Downtown ☎ 213-622 1966 🚍 DASH A, B ⊕ Mon, Wed & Fri 8am-noon, Tues, Thurs & Sat 6am-noon

FACTORY OUTLETS

The Cooper Building

(3, H4) At the heart of the Garment District since 1930, this grand old building houses more than 50 factory outlets, mostly selling designer brands.

✉ 860 S Los Angeles St, Downtown ☎ 213-627 3754 🚍 DASH A, B ⊕ Mon-Sat 9.30am-5.30pm, Sun 11am-5pm

CLOTHING & JEWELLERY

Aardvark's

The definitive second-hand clothing store in an area where nearly all threads

are 'pre-owned'.

✉ 7579 Melrose Ave, Hollywood (4, D3) ☎ 323-655 6769 🚍 MTA 3, 10 ⊕ Mon-Thurs & Sun 11am-7pm, Fri-Sat 11am-9pm

Curve

Curve design and make their own extremely tasteful, modern clothing for both sexes. Reasonably priced for the quality.

✉ 154 N Robertson, West Hollywood (4, G2) ☎ 310-360 8008 🚍 MTA 3 or 10, then walk south on Robertson ⊕ 11am-7pm

Fox Jewelry Plaza

One of the many jewellery bargain centres in this area, with prices up to 70% less than elsewhere in the city. Not all of the offerings are of the best quality, so shop with care.

✉ 608 S Hill St, Jewelry District (3, G3) ☎ 213-627 8907 🚍 DASH A, B ⊕ Mon-Fri 9am-6pm

SLOW

If you can't find a whacky retro outfit or Hawaiian shirt here, you're in trouble.

✉ 7474 Melrose Ave, W Hollywood (4, D3) ☎ 323-655 3725

🚇 MTA 10 🕐 Mon-Sat
11.30am-9pm, Sun
11am-8pm

Star Wares on Main
Find Geena Davis hand-
me-downs and jeans that
John Travolta outgrew at
this star-studded second-
hand store.
✉ 2817 Main St,
Santa Monica (2, D1)
☎ 310-399 0224
🚇 MTA 33; SM 1
🕐 10.30am-6pm

ART & ANTIQUES
Antiquarius
Right near the Pacific
Design Center, it has over
40 antique shops with
especially good selections
of jewellery and silver.
✉ 8840 Beverly Blvd,
W Hollywood (4, G2)
☎ 310-274 2363
🚇 MTA 14 🕐 Mon-Sat
10am-6pm, Sun 12-6pm

The Antique Guild
Held in the historic Helms
Bakery building, this major
antique market covers 2
acres; enthusiasts should
allow an entire day to
browse.
✉ 8800 Venice Blvd,
Culver City (4, H5)
☎ 310-838 3131
🚇 SM 12 🕐 Mon-Sat
10am-6pm, Sun 12-6pm

Rose Bowl Flea
Market (2, B5)
Held in the grounds of the
1922-era Rose Bowl stadi-
um, this flea market offers
undeniably good people-
watching and one of the
best places to look for
deals. A pleasant way to
while away the morning.
✉ 1001 Rose Bowl Dr,
Pasadena ☎ 323-560
7469 🚇 MTA 180, 181
🕐 2nd Sunday of the
month, 9am-3pm

Funky Melrose Avenue is lined with unique boutique

GALLERIES
Bergamot Station
This former trolley station
now houses a 26,000 sq ft
collection of very nice galleries that deal in everything from contemporary
glass work to photography.
✉ 2525 Michigan Ave,
Santa Monica (2, D1)
☎ 310-829 5854 🚇
SM 9 🚗 Santa Monica
(10) Fwy to Cloverfield
exit 🕐 Tues-Fri 10am-
5pm, Sat 11am-5pm

Gideon Gallery
An intriguing collection of
16th-19th century etchings
and lithographs.
✉ 8748 Melrose Ave,
W Hollywood (4, G2)
☎ 310-657 4194 🚇
MTA 10 🕐 Mon-Fri
9am-5pm

Margo Leavin
Gallery
Specialising in serious con-
temporary international art,
including pieces by Claes
Oldenburg and Alexis
Smith.
✉ 812 N Robertson
Blvd, W Hollywood (4,
G2) ☎ 213-273 0603
🚇 MTA 4, 220 🕐
Mon-Fri 9am-6pm

MUSIC & BOOKS
A-1 Record Finders
If you can't find it any-
where else and are willing
to wait a day or so while
they locate it, you can get
just about any piece of
recorded music.
✉ 5639 Melrose Ave,
W Hollywood (4, B3)
☎ 323-732 6737 🚇
MTA 10 🕐 Mon-Sat
10am-10pm

Arcana
Shelf upon shelf of art,
design and architecture
books are found at this
stylish bookstore.
✉ 1250 Third St
Promenade, Santa
Monica (2, D1) ☎ 310-
458 1499 🚇 MTA 20,
22; SM 1, 2, 7, 8, 9, 10
🕐 Mon-Sat 10am-6pm,
Sun 12-6pm

Bodhi's Books
An enormous selection of
New Age, religious, lifestyle
and spirituality books, plus
lectures and herbal reme-
dies. Used books are sold
in the annex at the rear.
✉ 8585 Melrose Ave,
W Hollywood (4, F2) ☎
310-659 1733 🚇 MTA
10 🕐 10am-11pm

Book Soup
A good place to find international magazines and newspapers, it draws students and celebrities to its eclectic assortment of titles, including a large gay & lesbian collection.
✉ 8818 Sunset Blvd, W Hollywood (4, F1) ☎ 310-659 3110 🚌 MTA 2, 3 ⏰ 9am-midnight

Form Zero
In a Gehry-designed complex on Santa Monica's Main St, the space is as aesthetically pleasing as the art books sold within.
✉ 2435 Main St, Santa Monica (2, D1) ☎ 310-450 0222 🚌 SM 1 ⏰ Mon-Thurs 10.30am-7pm, Fri-Sat 10.30am-9pm, Sun 11.30am-6pm

Tower Records
The original of what claims to be the largest music store chain on the planet. There are 2 shops here: one for classical music and videos, the other for everything else.
✉ 8801 Sunset Blvd, W Hollywood (4, F1) ☎ 310-657 7300 🚌 MTA 2 ⏰ 9am-midnight

FOOD & DRINK
Farmers Market
See page 72.

Grand Central Market (3, F3)
A Downtown LA institution since 1917, Grand Central has around 50 vendors who hawk fresh fruits and vegetables, meat and seafood, hand-tossed tortillas, and home-made Chinese noodles.
✉ 317 S Broadway ☎ 323-624 2378 🚌 DASH D ⏰ Mon-Sat 9am-6pm, Sun 10am-5.30pm

The Wine Merchant
Rare vintages, tastings and classes are presided over by Dennis Overstreet, a legend in the trade.
✉ cnr Lt Santa Monica Blvd & N Roxbury Dr, Beverly Hills (4, J2) ☎ 310-278 7322 🚌 MTA 4 ⏰ Mon-Sat 10am-6pm

SPECIALTY STORES
Collectors Book Store
An essential stop for film aficionados, with its inventory of film memorabilia, including old scripts, movie posters and publicity stills.
✉ 1708 N Vine St, Hollywood (4, B3) ☎ 323-467 3296 🚌 MTA 1 ⏰ 10am-5pm (Sat till 5.30pm)

Golden Apple
Comics, sci-fi, Japanimation and more in the form of toys, mags, books, model kits and other collectibles.
✉ 7711 Melrose Ave, W Hollywood (4, D3) ☎ 323-658 6047 🚌 MTA 10 ⏰ Mon-Sat 10am-9pm, Sun 11am-7pm

Kate Spade
Exquisite handbags at over-the-top prices.
✉ 105 S Robertson Blvd, W Hollywood (4, G2) ☎ 310-271 9778

🚌 MTA 220 ⏰ Mon-Sat 10am-6pm, Sun 12-5pm

LA County Hall of Administraton
The county coroner department's bizarre Skeletons in the Closet gift shop sells items such as beach towels with chalk outlines to benefit the city's Youth Drunk Driving Program.
✉ cnr Temple & Hill Sts, Downtown (3, E3) ☎ 323-343 0786 🚌 MTA 78 ⏰ Mon-Fri 8am-4.30pm

Modernica
Come here to find out what's up-and-coming in the world of design, even if you're not in the market to buy.
✉ 7366 Beverly Blvd, W Hollywood (4, D3) ☎ 323-933 0383 🚌 MTA 2 14, 316 ⏰ Mon-Fri 10am-6pm, Sat 11am-6pm, Sun 12-5pm

Waterworks
Just the place to buy bubble baths, bath oils, sponges and other treats to pamper yourself. Even the packaging is luxurious here.
✉ 109 S Robertson Blvd, W Hollywood (4, G2) ☎ 310-246 9766 🚌 MTA 220; SM 12 ⏰ Mon-Sat 11am-7pm, Sun 12-5pm

Super Dooper Supermarkets
A trip to California would not be complete without a look at the vast quantity of goods on the shelves of American supermarkets. Ralph's, Vons, Lucky, Safeway, Albertsons and Alpha Beta are all chain-owned food stores that have a deli, bakery, meat and seafood counter, pharmacy, florist, office supplies, greeting cards, beach chairs, ice coolers, coffee makers and take-away sushi. These stores are often open 24hrs a day, or at least until 10pm.

SAN FRANCISCO & BAY AREA

Big department stores and international name-brand boutiques gather around **Union Square** (7, D4) and the streets between it and the Financial District. For San Francisco souvenirs there's no better – or worse – place than **Pier 39**, Fisherman's Wharf (7, B1), or Chinatown's **Grant Ave** (7, C3).

Haight St (7, H3) is a youth-culture mecca. It's an especially good area for vintage clothing and music (especially older and second-hand CDs and vinyl). In the Mission District, **Valencia St** (7, G5), especially between 16th and 24th Sts, is a hot spot for recycled clothing and second-hand furniture.

Castro St (7, J5), just south of Market St, is one of the most vibrant shopping neighbourhoods. It has a bit of everything – chi chi antique shops, men's clothing stores, bookshops, novelty stores, 'lotion & potion' vendors – aimed partly at an affluent gay crowd. Follow Castro St south (or take the Muni J streetcar) to Noe Valley's **24th St** (6, E5), a thoroughly San Franciscan street packed with a fine selection of clothes, books and food, plus a preponderance of shops selling maternity wear, recycled kids' clothes, and toys.

Berkeley's **Telegraph Ave** has hand-made jewellery and one of the nation's biggest and best concentrations of books and music. Berkeley's north side – along Shattuck Ave north of University Ave – is called the **'gourmet ghetto'** for its wine, cheese and specialty food shops.

SHOPPING MALLS

The Cannery (7, C1)
A small group of whimsical stores in the brick structure that used to house the Del Monte fruit-canning factory.
✉ 2801 Leavenworth St, Fisherman's Wharf
☎ 415-771 3112 🚌 Muni 30, 32, 42 🚃 Powell-Hyde cable car

🕐 most shops Mon-Sat 10am-6pm, Sun 12-6pm

Ghirardelli Square (7, D1) Housed in the old Ghirardelli chocolate factory, the square houses a collection of shops and boutiques (including a terrific kite store) around an outdoor plaza.

✉ 900 North Point St, Fisherman's Wharf ☎ 415-775 5500 🚌 Muni 19 🚃 Powell-Hyde cable car 🕐 most shops Tues-Fri 10am-8pm, Sat 10am-7pm, Sun 10am-6pm

Pier 39 (7, B1)
This remodelled working pier is the place to buy replicas of the Golden Gate Bridge, 'My Grandmother went to Alcatraz and all she brought me is this stupid T-shirt!' T-shirts and other tacky memoirs. It's a festive place, with restaurants, quirky 'museums', troops of photogenic sea lions and a Venetian carousel for the kids.
✉ Fisherman's Wharf ☎ 415-981 7437 🚌 Muni 19 🚃 Powell-Mason cable car 🕐 Mon-Thurs & Sun 10am-6pm, Fri-Sat 10am-10pm; June-Sept 10am-10pm daily

Ghirardelli started a national trend when it converted its chocolate factory into a shopping centre.

John Elk III

San Francisco Shopping Center

A stylish collection of high-end stores surrounding a voluminous vertical space and topped by Nordstrom's. A huge new Bloomingdale's is scheduled to open next door to the centre in 2001.

✉ 865 Market St, SoMa (7, D4) ☎ 415-495 5656 🚇 🚇 BART or Muni to Powell St 🚇 Muni 9 ⏰ 10am-9pm

DEPARTMENT STORES

Macy's

Plush department store complex with several buildings on and around Union Square. Its holiday window decorations are fabulous.

✉ cnr O'Farrell & Stockton Sts, Union Square (7, D4) ☎ 415-397 3333 🚇 🚇 BART or Muni to Powell St 🚇 Muni 2, 3, 4 ⏰ Mon-Sat 10am-8pm, Sun 11am-7pm

ump's – a San Francisco institution (p. 67)

Neiman Marcus

The glass-domed lobby of Neiman-Marcus' classic 1920s building brings light to all levels of this high-end department store.

✉ 150 Stockton St, Union Square (7, D4) ☎ 415-362 3900 🚇 BART Powell St 🚇 Muni 2, 3, 4 ⏰ Mon-Sat 10am-7pm, Thurs 10am-8pm, Sun 12-6pm

Saks Fifth Avenue

The north-west anchor to Union Square and an old-time San Francisco favourite for its designer make-up, clothes and jewellery.

✉ 384 Post St, Union Square (7, D4) ☎ 415-986 4300 🚇 BART Powell St 🚇 Muni 2, 3, 4 🚇 Powell St cable cars ⏰ Mon-Sat 10am-7pm, Sun 12-7pm

FACTORY OUTLETS

Esprit Factory Outlet

A big warehouse with 30-50% discounts on Esprit apparel, bags and shoes.

✉ 499 Illinois St at 16th St, Potrero Hill (6, C4) ☎ 415-957 2550 🚇 Muni 15 ⏰ Mon-Fri 10am-8pm, Sat 10am-7pm, Sun 11am-6pm

ART & ANTIQUES

Galerie Adrienne

This 3-storey gallery is conservative in its purchases, but the result is a fine-tuned collection of international and US contemporary art. A few older pieces can be found among the modern mix.

✉ cnr Sutter & Powell Sts, Union Square (7, D4) ☎ 415-288 6575 🚇 BART Powell St 🚇 Muni 2, 3, 4 ⏰ Mon-Wed 10am-6pm, Thurs-Sat 9am-8pm, Sun 12-5pm

Minna St Gallery

Great gallery with a small coffee bar that gives a decent perspective on the alternative San Francisco art scene.

✉ 111 Minna St, SoMa (7, C5) ☎ 415-974 1719 🚇 BART Montgomery St 🚇 Muni 14, 26; Sam Trans 5M, 7B 🚇 Market St Muni lines ⏰ Tues-Fri 1-7pm, Sat 4-7pm

Nevska Gallery

Russian art and iconography at way-out prices.

✉ 353 Geary St, Union Square (7, D4) ☎ 415-392 4932 🚇 Muni 38 ⏰ Sun-Wed 9.30am-

Levi Strauss

San Francisco's most famous contribution to sartorial elegance is Levi's jeans. A German gold-rush immigrant, 21-year-old Levi Strauss, arrived from New York in 1850 burdened with materials from his brother's store. When he'd sold everything except the sailcloth, he struck on the idea of using it to make indestructible pants for hard-working miners. With his brothers he founded Levi's in 1853 and in 1873 their famous riveted pockets idea was patented. Even the word 'denim' was a Levi Strauss invention: when *serge* fabric from Nîmes, France, was substituted for the original sailcloth, the phrase *'serge de Nîmes'* (serge from Nîmes) became 'denim'.

5.30pm, Thurs-Sat
10.30am-9.30pm

CLOTHING & JEWELLERY
Asphalt
A large selection of hip men's and women's wear by local designers.
✉ 551 Hayes St at Octavia, Hayes Valley (7, F4) ☎ 415-626 5196 🚇 Muni 21 ⊘ Mon-Sat 12-7pm, Sun 1-5pm

---

San Fran Style
The Gap, a San Francisco-based clothing company, has half a dozen city locations, the most prominent being the flagship store (☎ 415-788 5909) in the James Flood Building at the corner of Market and Powell Sts (7, D4). **Banana Republic**, a more up-market version of The Gap, has stores at 256 Grant Ave (7, D4; ☎ 415-788 3087) and 2 Embarcadero Center (7, C4; ☎ 415-986 5076).

Community Thrift Store
Densely packed with good used stuff in a neighbourhood full of thrift stores.
✉ 625 Valencia St, The Mission (7, G5) ☎ 415-861 4910 🚇 16th & Mission 🚇 Muni 14, 26 ⊘ 10am-6.30pm

Guys & Dolls
A hidden-away gem with lots of clothes and accessories from the 1930s and 40s, this is a necessary stop before going swing dancing.
✉ 4789 24th St, Noe

Valley (6, E5) ☎ 415-285 7174 🚇 Muni J ⊘ Mon-Fri 11am-7pm, Sat 11am-6pm, Sun 12-6pm

Jeremy's
A good place to find a discounted Hugo Boss suit, Armani pants or Laundry dress. Flawed and surplus stock arrive daily from retail shops, so you never know what you'll find.
✉ 2 South Park Ave, SoMa (6, C3) ☎ 415-882 4929 🚇 BART Montgomery St 🚇 Muni 15 ⊘ Mon-Fri 11am-7pm, Sat 11am-6pm, Sun 11am-5pm

MUSIC & BOOKS
A Different Light Bookstore
America's largest gay and lesbian bookseller, it holds author readings most nights from 7.30pm.
✉ 489 Castro St, The Castro (7, J4) ☎ 415-431 0891 🚇 Muni 33, 24 🚇 Muni K, L, M ⊘ 10am-midnight

City Lights
Heart and soul of the Beat movement, City Lights was the first paperbacks-only bookshop in the country. It still stocks rare Allen Ginsberg and Jack Kerouac selections.
✉ 261 Columbus Ave, North Beach (7, C3) ☎ 415-362 8193 🚇 Muni 15 ⊘ 10am-midnight

Staceys Bookstore
Three floors of new books (they claim over 100,000 titles!) plus a mezzanine with magazines and international newspapers. Authors give readings several times a week.
✉ 581 Market St, Union Square (7, D4)

☎ 415-421 4687 🚇 BART Montgomery St 🚇 Muni 6, 7, 21 ⊘ Mon-Fri 8.30am-7pm, Sat 9am-6.30pm, Sun 11am-5pm

Virgin Megastore
You can easily spend half a day in this monstrous music store, complete with listening stations and a cafe.
✉ 2 Stockton St at Market, Union Square (7, D4) ☎ 415-397 4525 🚇 BART Powell St 🚇 Muni 30, 45 ⊘ Mon-Thurs 9am-11pm, Fri-Sat 9am-midnight, Sun 9am-10pm

OUTDOOR & TRAVEL GEAR
Eddie Bauer
If you envisage yourself paddling a canoe across a pristine lake to where a dog, handsome spouse and rustic cabin await, head to this store for 3 floors of yuppified outdoor equipment and clothing.
✉ 220 Post St, Union Square (7, D4) ☎ 415-986 7600 🚇 BART Montgomery St 🚇 Muni 2, 3, 4 ⊘ Mon-Fri 10am-8pm, Sat-Sun 11am-6pm

The North Face
A good selection of high-quality outdoor and adventure travel gear, though you may get better deals at their **factory outlet** store at 1325 Howard St, SoMa (7, F5; ☎ 415-626 6444).
✉ 180 Post St, Union Square (7, D4) ☎ 415-433 3223 🚇 BART Montgomery St 🚇 Muni 2, 3, 4 ⊘ Mon-Sat 10am-8pm, Sun 11am-6pm

Patagonia

A beautifully designed shop selling good quality Patagonia outdoor and travel gear.

✉ 770 North Point St, Fisherman's Wharf (7, C1) ☎ 415-771 2050 🚌 Muni 19 🚋 Powell-Hyde cable car ◷ Mon-Wed & Sat 10am-6pm, Thurs-Fri 10am-8pm, Sun 11am-5pm

FOOD & DRINK
Boudin Bakery

A chain bakery popular with tourists, Boudin is still the best place for classic San Francisco sourdough.

✉ 156 Jefferson St, Fisherman's Wharf (7, C1) ☎ 415-928 1849 🚌 Muni 19 🚋 Powell-Hyde cable car ◷ 7.30am-late

Boudin Bakery, the San Francisco sourdough specialists

Ghirardelli's Premium Chocolates

You can find Ghirardelli treats all over the city and beyond, but to make an experience of it, check out this store in the namesake square. A second shop, Ghirardelli Too (☎ 415-474 1414), is also in the square. But if all you're after is their chocolate bars, head to Walgreens where they're much cheaper.

✉ Ghiradelli Square (7, D1) ☎ 415-474 3938 🚌 Muni 19 🚋 Powell-Hyde cable car ◷ Sun-Thurs

10.30am-11.30pm, Fri-Sat 10.30am-midnight

Napa Valley Winery Exchange

The exchange stocks small production and specialty wines from all over California, but especially from the Napa Valley.

✉ 415 Taylor St at Geary St, Union Square (7, D4) ☎ 415-771 2887 🚌 Muni 38 ◷ Mon-Sat 10am-7pm

Plump Jack Wines

Just the place to get excellent recommendations and fair prices on all varieties of wine.

✉ cnr Fillmore & Greenwich Sts, Cow Hollow (6, F2) ☎ 415-346 9870 🚌 Muni 22 ◷ Mon-Sat 11am-8pm, Sun 11am-6pm

SPECIALTY STORES
Adolph Gasser

Has a huge range of new and used photographic and video equipment, and also processes film.

✉ 181 2nd St, SoMa (7, C5) ☎ 415-495 3852 🚇 BART Montgomery St 🚌 Muni 14 ◷ Mon-Sat 9am-6pm

Cliff's Variety

Here you can find anything from Play-Doh to that nail you need to hang your SFMOMA poster.

✉ 479 Castro St, The Castro (7, J4) ☎ 415-431 5365 🚌 Muni 33, 24 🚋 Muni to Castro St ◷ Mon-Sat 9.30am-8pm (linen dept 10am-7pm)

Gump's

A San Francisco institution, Gump's is half museum, half homewares emporium. Crystal, china, silver and unique gifts are on offer.

✉ 135 Post St, Union Square (7, D4) ☎ 415-982 1616 🚇 BART Montgomery St 🚌 any down Market St ◷ Mon-Sat 10am-6pm

SFO Snowboarding & FTC Skateboarding

State-of-the-art snow-boards and skateboards, plus all the cool gear that goes with them.

✉ 618 Shrader St, Upper Haight (7, J2) ☎ 415-386 1666 🚌 Muni 8 🚋 Muni N ◷ Tues-Sun 10am-6pm

Outlet Malls

Outlet malls should be approached with caution. While bargains can be found, goods are often damaged, irregular or last season's fashion. At more upscale outlet malls prices are often marked up before they're reduced, so stock is actually no cheaper than retail. Service at the malls is minimal, as are dressing rooms and mirrors.

SAN DIEGO

The **Spanish Village** area of Balboa Park is a good place to find paintings (mostly watercolours) of the San Diego area. If you make a trip to Escondido or Carlsbad, locally-grown **produce**, such as dates, avocados, citrus fruit and wine, can be bought for reasonable prices. A uniquely San Diegan gift would be anything emblazoned with the logo of a local surf shop. Every museum and visitor attraction has a gift shop, so souvenir hunters might find a stuffed Shamu (the celebrity killer whale) at Sea World, a realistic rubber snake at the zoo, or an old photo at the Museum of San Diego History.

You can make a fun day of mall-hopping by trolley: start downtown at Horton Plaza (9, E3), take the San Diego Trolley Blue Line to Old Town (for lunch and margaritas), then continue on the Blue Line to the triad of malls – Fashion Valley, the Hazard Center and Mission Valley Center – in Mission Valley (8, E4).

SHOPPING MALLS

Fashion Valley (8, E4)
Specialty stores like Tiffany & Co, Enzo Antolini and Restoration Hardware plus biggies like Saks Fifth Ave, Macy's and Nordstrom.
✉ **7007 Friars Rd, Mission Valley** ☎ 619-688 9113 🚌 MTS 6, 13, 16, 20, 20A, 20B, 25, 27, 41, 81, 990 🚃 **Blue Line to Fashion Valley** ⊘ most stores 10am-10pm

Horton Plaza (9, E3)
A big postmodern mall with cinemas, theatres, restaurants and 140 shops in a wildly colourful, crescent-shaped open courtyard – it's like an Escher drawing come to life.
✉ **Gaslamp Quarter** ☎ 619-238 1596 🚌 MTS to Gaslamp Quarter ⊘ Mon-Fri 10am-9pm, Sat 10am-6pm, Sun 11am-6pm

University Towne Center (8, B3)
Good despite its rather pretentious name. Boutiques and chain stores open onto an outdoor cor- ridor lined with fountains where bronze dolphins swim and spout. There's also a food court, Olympic-sized ice skating rink, movie theatre and child-care centre.
✉ **cnr Genesee Ave and La Jolla Village Dr, La Jolla** ☎ 858-546 8858 🚌 MTS 5, 21, 30, 31, 34, 34B, 41, 50, 150, 301, 310 ⊘ Mon-Fri 10am-9pm, Sat 10am-8pm, Sun 11am-7pm

Colourful Horton Plaza

James Lyon

FACTORY OUTLETS

North County Factory Outlet Center
Discount outlets for Nike, Levi's, Bass and other big names; not all prices are bargains, so shop carefully.
✉ **1050 Los Vallecitos Blvd, San Marcos (1, J7)** ☎ 619-595 5222 🚌 MTS 304 ⊘ Mon-Thurs 10am-7pm, Fri-Sat 10am-8pm, Sun 11am-6pm

MARKETS

Kobey's Swap Meet
Massive flea market in the parking lot of the San Diego Sports Arena. Used sports goods, books, T-shirts and car parts are especially abundant.
✉ **San Diego Sports Arena, 3350 Sports Arena Blvd (8, F3)** ☎ 619-226 0650 🚌 MTS 26, 34 ⊘ Thurs-Sun 7am-3pm

ART & ANTIQUES

Cedros Ave Design District
Four blocks of unique art and architecture studios, antique stores and hand-crafted clothing boutiques.

✉ **Cedros Ave, Solana Beach (1, K7)** 🚆 **Amtrak/Coaster from downtown to Solana Beach station** 🚌 **MTS 308, 310**

Newport Ave (8, F2)
Ocean Beach's main drag is well stocked with surf shops, music stores, used-clothing places and, in the 4800 and 4900 blocks, antique-consignment stores.
🚌 **MTS 23, 35** ⏰ **most stores 10am-6pm**

Spanish Village Art Center
Watch potters, jewellers, glass blowers, painters and sculptors churn out pricey but unique decorative items.
✉ **Balboa Park (off map)** ⏰ **11am-4pm** 🚌 **MTS 7, 7A, 7B, 15, 20, 20A, 20B, 115, 210, 270, 560, 810, 820, 850**

BOOKS
Bay Books
International newspapers, a vast selection of best-sellers and an espresso bar – what more could you want?
✆ **1029 Orange Ave, Coronado (8, H3)** ☎ **935-435 0070** 🚌 **MTS 901-904** ⏰ **Mon-Thurs 8am-8pm, Sat 8am-9pm**

DG Wills
An outstanding selection of used, rare and out-of-print books.
✉ **7461 Girard Ave, La Jolla (8, C1)** ☎ **858-456 1800** 🚌 **MTS 30, 34, 34A, 34B** ⏰ **10am-8pm**

SPECIALTY SHOPS
Babette Schwartz
Named for its owner (queen of the local drag scene), this store sells icons of past and present popular culture, along with odd and X-rated greeting cards. Be prepared to laugh.
✉ **421 University Ave, Hillcrest (8, F4)** ☎ **619-220 7048** 🚌 **MTS 1, 8, 11, 16** ⏰ **Mon-Thurs 10am-9pm, Fri-Sat 10am-9.30pm, Sun 10am-6pm**

FOOD & DRINK
Bread & Cie
Hand-baked breads sold by the loaf, slice or made into a sandwich.
✉ **350 University Ave, Hillcrest (8, F4)** ☎ **619-683 9322** 🚌 **MTS 1, 8, 11, 16** ⏰ **Mon-Fri 7am-7pm, Sat 7am-6pm, Sun 8am-6pm**

The Cheese Shop
An interesting array of imported items (chutneys, biscuits, candy) accompanies excellent deli items and baked goods; locals love their sandwiches.
✉ **cnr 4th Ave & G St, Gaslamp Quarter (9, E4)** ☎ **619-232 2303** 🚌 **MTS 1, 3, 5, 16, 25** ⏰ **Mon-Fri 7am-5pm, Sat 8am-4pm, Sun 8am-3pm**

OB People's Market
An organic co-op with bulk foods and an excellent deli.
✉ **cnr Voltaire St & Sunset Cliffs Blvd, Ocean Beach (8, F2)** ☎ **619-224 1387** 🚌 **MTS 23, 35** ⏰ **8am-9pm**

Point Loma Seafoods
A market-cum-deli that's one of the liveliest local places for seafood, fresh bread, beer and wine.
✉ **2805 Emerson St, Shelter Island Marina (8, G2)** ☎ **619-223 1109** 🚌 **MTS 22, 23, 28** ⏰ **market: 9am-7pm; kitchen: 10.30am-7pm; both from noon on Sunday**

The Wine Bank
Housed in a historic brownstone building, this no-nonsense wine shop has varieties from every region of every major wine-producing country, and staff who know their grapes.
✉ **363 5th Ave, Gaslamp Quarter (9, E4)** ☎ **619-234 7487** 🚌 **MTS 1, 3, 4, 5, 16, 25** ⏰ **Mon-Fri 10am-8pm, Sat 11am-5pm**

San Diego's Farmers Markets
The street performers and food vendors that frequent the **OB Farmers Market** in Newport Ave, Ocean Beach (8, F2) make it San Diego's most enjoyable. It's held every Wednesday from 4-7pm (until 8pm June-Sept). On Sunday from 9am-noon **Hillcrest's Farmers Market**, on the corner of Normal and Lincoln Sts (8, F4), is a fun place to people-watch and buy fresh produce. Also on Sunday morning is the **La Jolla Farmer's Market**, at La Jolla Elementary on the south end of Girard Ave (8, C1), where $10 massages, jewellery and gourmet picnic items (breads, cheeses, smoked fish) sell as well as fresh produce and flowers. Live jazz sets the scene.

AROUND CALIFORNIA

Coachella Valley   (1, J8)

High-class boutiques, art galleries and antique stores can be found along El Paseo in **Palm Desert**. B Lewin Galleries (☎ 760-325 7611), 210 S Palm Canyon Dr, has an extensive collection of paintings by top Mexican artists.

The Desert Fashion Plaza (☎ 760-320 8282), 123 N Palm Canyon Dr, has a number of upscale fashion outlets. Lots of stores in downtown **Palm Springs** sell 'resort wear' – light, bright casual clothes.

Monterey Peninsula   (1, F4)

Chain shops are banned in central **Carmel** although European chains like Benetton and Crabtree & Evelyn seem exempt. Carmel galleries are laden with happy dolphin sculptures and local scenery oil paintings. The Carmel Art Association (☎ 831-624 6176) on Dolores St presents works by local artists. The Weston Gallery (☎ 831-624 4453) on 6th Ave, between Dolores and Lincoln, offers some excellent photographic work.

University Stores

For authentic logo sweatshirts, hats, notebooks, pencils and cups, head to the student union store of any college or university campus. University of California (Berkeley, LA, Santa Barbara, San Diego) items are especially popular and of good quality.

The Redwoods   (1, B2)

Numerous roadside stands sell all sorts of 'stuff' made from redwood and redwood burls. Small boxes made of the wood are usually of fine quality and give anything kept inside them a wonderful smell.

Santa Barbara   (1, H5)

Paseo Nuevo, between Cañon Perdido and Ortega Sts, is a charming outdoor mall with Nordstrom and Robinsons-May department stores, and various chain stores. **La Arcada**, 1114 State St at Figueroa St, is a historic red-tiled arcade designed by Myron Hunt (builder of Rose Bowl stadium in LA) and filled with boutiques, restaurants and public art. Another lovely, flower-festooned courtyard is the **Historic Paseo**, opposite Paseo Nuevo. **State St** shops sell clothing, knick-knacks, antiques and books.

Wine Country   (5, A3)

California wine is a terrific gift. The Napa and Sonoma valley area

Some of the best wines in the world come from the Wine Country.

(p. 30) produces the best wines overall, though the Anderson Valley has terrific chardonnays and Amador County produces fine zinfandels and syrahs. Most well-known Napa and Sonoma Valley wines are cheaper at liquor stores, though tasting and buying from the winery has its own charm. Smaller wineries rarely distribute their wares outside their vineyard.

places to eat

Californiaʼs dining scene is as diverse as its population. It is possible to eat Mexican *huevos rancheros* for breakfast, a Thai curry for lunch, and Indian thali for dinner, without venturing out of one neighbourhood. Even one-horse towns are likely to have at least one Mexican and one Chinese restaurant. Smoking is prohibited in all restaurants (even bars).

California Cuisine

The mid-1980s gourmet movement, led by Alice Waters, Wolfgang Puck and Nancy Waters, established a definable California cuisine which revolves around fresh, seasonal ingredients, innovative combinations and artistic presentation. Low-fat ingredients and cooking methods are a big part of California cuisine, but by no means define it. Typical entrees might include angel-hair pasta with sun-dried tomatoes, garlic and fresh basil or braised chicken with sesame-ginger soy sauce.

The newest trend in upscale restaurants is Pacific Rim or Cal-Asian cooking, which combines local ingredients with traditional Asian techniques. Meat and fish seasoned with turmeric, fresh coriander, ginger, garlic and chilli land atop Asian staples like rice, sweet potatoes or buckwheat *udon* noodles. Appetisers are often especially fun; donʼt hesitate to order several small dishes and make them your entire meal.

Meal Costs
The price ranges used in this chapter indicate the cost, for one person, of a main dish, one accompaniment (salad, side dish, dessert) and a drink.

$	$10 and under
$$	$11-$15
$$$	$16-$20
$$$$	over $20

David Peevers

Bobʼs Big Boy in LA, a classic slice of American kitsch

Liquor

Most restaurants are fully licensed, though California law permits patrons to BYOB (bring your own beverage), as long as the restaurant allows it. Corkage fees can be high ($10-$20 at high-end restaurants), though at unlicensed modest eateries thereʼs usually no charge and you might even need to supply your own bottle opener!

Expect wine lists to have bottles ranging from $20 to more than $100. Some very good Californian wines – especially merlots, pinot noirs and chardonnays – retail for $6-$8, which translates to $12-$20 on a wine list. Wines by the glass are $4-$7 and can be of good quality.

Taxes & Tipping

Any restaurant meal will actually cost you around 25% more than the price of the food you eat, once you add sales tax and a tip. Tipping is left to your discretion and should reflect the quality of service, but 15% is considered the norm. Tipping is not expected at fast-food restaurants with counter service, or self-serve buffets.

LOS ANGELES

LA's dining scene is greatly influenced by its Pacific Rim culture and proximity to Mexico. It doesn't have the usual eating 'districts' you'll find in most big cities, so it's better to select a particular restaurant and book a table. If you're intent on menu browsing before eating, head to Melrose Ave, Santa Monica's Main St or Third St Promenade, or Pier Plaza, Hermosa Beach.

BEVERLY HILLS
Matsuhisa $$$
Japanese
It looks like a mom-and-pop sushi joint, but has a 40-page menu and incorporates Peruvian herbs with traditional Japanese dishes – wow!
✉ 129 N La Cienega Blvd (3, F3) ☎ 310-659 9639 🚌 MTA 105, 576 ⏲ lunch 11.45am-2.15pm, dinner 5.45-10.15pm ♿ OK

What to Wear
Restaurant dress codes are practically non-existent. A handful of restaurants will require a jacket, but virtually none asks that you wear a tie. That said, shoes and shirts are required *almost* everywhere.

CHINATOWN
Empress Pavilion $-$$
Chinese
Any Los Angeleno will tell you this is the best place in LA for dim sum. Sundays are especially crowded.
✉ 3rd fl, Bamboo Plaza, 988 N Hill St (3, B3) ☎ 213-617 9898 🚇 Union Station 🚌 DASH B ⏲ Mon-Fri 9am-2.30pm & 5-10pm, Sat-Sun 5-10pm ♿ yes

Philippe the Original

Philippe the Original $
American
Established in 1908 and the self-proclaimed home of the French-dip sandwich, this place has replaced the sawdust on the floor once – and only once. There's no table service, and you should come prepared to share a table with strangers.
✉ 1001 N Alameda St (3, C4) ☎ 213-628 3781 🚌 DASH B ⏲ 6am-10pm ♿ yes

DOWNTOWN
Canter's $
Jewish Deli
It's about as close to 'New Yawk' as LA gets, with know-it-all waitresses, an ancient interior and the best corned beef on rye this side of Staten Island.
✉ 419 N Fairfax Ave,

Downtown (4, E3) ☎ 213-651 2030 🚌 MTA 14, 217 ⏲ 24hrs ♿ yes; special menu V

Farmers Market $-$$
Produce Market
An institution that began in 1934, the stalls at the open-air market sell hot and cold items, from sticky buns to dried shrimp balls. Brunching is popular – try Kokomo's.
✉ 6333 W 3rd St (4, F3) ☎ 323-933 9211 🚌 MTA 16, 217 ⏲ Mon-Sat 9am-7pm, Sun 10am-6pm ♿ yes V

Original Pantry Café $
American
Mayor Richard Riordan's cafe is open 24hrs and serves artery-clogging American meals that went out with bobby socks. Need bacon and eggs or a platter-sized steak at 3am? This is the place.
✉ cnr S Figueroa & 9th Sts (3, H2) ☎ 213-972 0187 🚌 DASH A, B ⏲ 24 hrs ♿ kids' menu

HOLLYWOOD & WEST HOLLYWOOD
Campanile $$$
Southern French
Under a glass roof covering the courtyard of a 1928 Spanish home once owned by Charlie Chaplin, this place has fine Southern French creations and a bakery that rates among LA's best. Bookings required.

✉ 624 S La Brea Ave, Hollywood (4, D4) ☎ 323-938 1447 🚌 MTA 10 ⏰ lunch Mon-Fri 11.30am-2pm, dinner Mon-Thurs 6-10pm, Fri-Sat 5.30-11pm, brunch Sat-Sun 9.30am-1.30pm ♿ yes

Patina $$$
French

Many Los Angelenos consider this French restaurant the city's single best dining experience. Joachim Splichal, the superstar chef, gets more accolades than most of his customers who saunter down from nearby Paramount Studios.

✉ 5955 Melrose Ave, Hollywood (4, C3) ☎ 323-467 1108 🚌 MTA 10, 11 ⏰ lunch Tues 12-2pm, dinner Sun-Thurs 6-9.30pm, Fri 6-10.30pm, Sat 5.30-10.30pm ♿ OK; earlier is better

Pink's Famous Chili Dogs $
American Fast Food

People queue day and night to grab a dog, fries and onion rings from this LA institution that's been around since 1939. It's the place most likely to feed celebrity hangovers.

✉ 709 N La Brea Ave, W Hollywood (4, D3) ☎ 323-931 4223 🚌 MTA 10, 11 ⏰ Sun-Thurs 9.30am-2am, Fri-Sat 9.30am-3am ♿ perfect!

Roscoe's House of Chicken & Waffles $
American

An odd combo that's won the hearts of many. You don't *have* to eat the chicken and waffles together, but converts claim that once you do, you'll never look back.

✉ 1514 N Gower St,

Hollywood (4, B2) ☎ 323-466 7453 🚌 MTA 2, 3, 323 ⏰ Sun-Thurs 8.30am-midnight, Fri-Sat 8.30am-4am

Spago $$$
Californian

Wolfgang Puck is the quintessential LA chef and this remains his, and arguably the city's, landmark fine dining establishment. If you eat at only one monumental restaurant, make it this one – and book ahead. Suit jackets required.

✉ 1114 Horn Ave, W Hollywood (4, F1) ☎ 310-385 0880 🚌 MTA 20, 21, 320 ⏰ lunch 11.30am-2.15pm, dinner 5.30-10.30pm ♿ OK

Yamashiro $$$
Cal-Japanese

The stunning views of LA and elaborate gardens – which include a 600-year-old pagoda – have always been better than the food at this Japanese restaurant; still it's as popular as ever.

✉ 1999 N Sycamore Ave, Hollywood Hills (4, C1) ☎ 323-466 5125 ⏰ Sun-Thurs 5.30-10pm, Fri-Sat 5.30-11pm ♿ OK

SANTA MONICA & VENICE
Bamboo $$-$$$
Cuban

A 'backyard barbecue' ambience pervades, but don't be concerned. The tasty Cuban dishes – grilled pork, fish and beef, served with fragrant black beans, rice and fried bananas – are excellent. Be daring and order anything – you can't go wrong.

✉ 10835 Venice Blvd, Venice (2, D2) ☎ 310-287 0668 🚌 MTA 33 ⏰ 11am-11.30pm ♿ yes

Chinois on Main $$$-$$$$
Pacific Rim

Wolfgang Puck's restaurant is justly famous for putting east-west fusion food on the map. Ginger, garlic, seafood and curries abound, and the decor – by Wolfgang's wife Barbara – is as whimsically exotic as what comes out of the kitchen.

✉ 2709 Main St, Santa Monica (2, D1) ☎ 310-392 3037 🚌 MTA 33; SM 1 ⏰ lunch Wed-Fri 11.30am-2pm, dinner nightly 5.30pm-late ♿ yes

Jiaraff $$$
Rustic American/French

Josiah Critin and Raphael Lunetta entertain their ever-expanding and loyal following at this tiny Santa Monica eatery that many prefer for lunch.

✉ cnr Santa Monica Blvd & 5th St (2, D1) ☎ 310-917 6671 🚌 SM 1; MTA 4 ⏰ lunch Tues-Fri 12-2pm; dinner Tues-Thurs 6-10pm, Fri-Sat 6-11pm, Sun 5.30-9pm ♿ OK

Rockenwagner $$$
Californian

Seasonal ingredients reign at this European-influenced eatery whose relaxed vibe belies its importance to LA's culinary scene. Don't hold back when the bread basket comes around – the selection is delicious.

✉ 2435 Main St, Santa Monica (2, D1) ☎ 310-399 6504 🚌 MTA 33, 333, 436; SM 1 ⏰ lunch Thurs 11.30am-2.30pm, brunch Sun 10am-3pm, dinner nightly 6-10pm (Fri-Sat till 11pm) ♿ no **V**

Ye Olde King's Head $
British
Popular for darts, beer, Sunday-night karaoke and authentic British food, such as bangers, battered fish and, of course, chips.
✉ 116 Santa Monica Blvd, Santa Monica (2, D1) ☎ 310-451 1402 🚌 MTA 4, 304; SM 1, 10 🕓 10am-10pm (bar till 2am) ♿ better during the day

SOUTH BAY
The Bottle Inn $$$
Italian
A long-standing favourite that does pasta and salads like no one else; dinner is romantic, lunch is breezy on the patio. The wine list is surprisingly extensive – one of LA's best.
✉ 26 22nd St, Hermosa Beach (2, F2) ☎ 310-376 9595 🚌 MTA 439 🕓 lunch Mon-Fri 11.30am-2.30pm, dinner nightly 6pm-late ♿ yes

El Sombrero $
Mexican
The taco sauce, tostadas and copious burritos at Manhattan Beach's old-school Mexican restaurant draws loyal diners from all over LA.
✉ 1005 Manhattan Ave, Manhattan Beach (2, F2) ☎ 310-374 1366 🚌 MTA 439 🕓 Mon-Fri 11am-9.15pm, Sat-Sun 11am-10pm ♿ child serves available

Polly's on the Pier $
American
Listen to water lapping and watch the fishing fleet at Redondo Beach while eating a no-nonsense meal like grits and corned beef hash, or tuna melts for lunch. A steady local business for over 30 years.
✉ 233 N Harbor Dr, Redondo Beach (2, G2) ☎ 310-318 3736 🚌 MTA 130, 439 🕓 5am-2pm ♿ kid's meals

> ### Follow Suit
> For a bustling, energetic lunch scene, head to the business district of any city – like San Francisco Financial District – where the number of suit-clad munchers is an indication of the best & cheapest places to eat.

SAN FRANCISCO & BAY AREA

San Francisco has more restaurants per capita than any other city in the USA. Try the Richmond district for Chinese, North Beach for Italian or The Mission for Mexican and Latin American. The restaurants on Fillmore St, between Sutter and Jackson Sts (7, F2), blend Japanese with other cuisines. For Thai, Burmese and Indonesian, try the 2 blocks of Post St from Taylor to Leavenworth (7, E3).

BERKELEY (5, B3)
Chez Panisse $$$
Californian
For a world-famous temple of gastronomy (the Dalai Lama eats here when he's in town, no kidding), this place has retained a welcoming atmosphere. At the restaurant downstairs you're served phenomenal fixed price meals – pasta in shellfish broth, beef tenderloin with black truffles – while upstairs at the cafe it's more moderately priced à la carte fare. Alice Waters lovingly presides.
✉ 1517 Shattuck Ave

Chez Panisse

☎ 510-548 5525 📧 www.chezpanisse.com 🚇 BART Berkeley 🕓 cafe: Mon-Thurs 11.30am-3pm & 5-10pm, Fri-Sat 11.30am-4pm & 5-11.30pm; restaurant: Mon-Sat, by reservation only ♿ best in the cafe

Zachary's Pizza $$
Italian
People from Chicago rave about this Chicago-style pizza – stuffed with an array of fresh ingredients.
✉ 5801 College Ave ☎ 510-655 6385 🚇 BART Rockridge 🕓 Sun-

Thurs 10am-10pm, Fri-
Sat 10am-10.30pm V

DOWNTOWN SAN
FRANSISCO
Bix   SS-SSS
American
If Bogey and Bacall were
dining in SF, they'd certain-
ly come to this swanky
supper club; jazz, fabulous
martinis and balcony
booths set the scene.
✉ 56 Gold St, Jackson
Square (7, C3) ☎ 415-
433 6300 ⓦ BART
Embarcadero ◷ lunch
Mon-Fri 11.30am-
2.30pm, dinner nightly
6-10.30pm (Sun till
10pm) ⚲ no

Empress of
China   SS-SSS
Chinese
A complete contrast to
Chinatown's cheap dives.
Splashy Chinese decor,
splendid views of the bay
and city and top-notch traditional Chinese food, with
nothing too spicy or exotic
on the menu.
✉ 838 Grant Ave,
Chinatown (7, C3) ☎
415-434 1345 ⓦ Muni
15, 30, 45 ◷ lunch
11am-2.45pm, dinner
5pm-late ⚲ OK V

ditional Chinatown fare

Postrio   SSSS
Californian
Prime exponent of
California cuisine, as
dreamt up by Wolfgang
Puck and executed by
Mitchell and Steven
Rosenthal. It always get
raves and never comes up
short, according to those in
the know.
✉ Prescott Hotel, 545
Post St, Union Square
(7, D4) ☎ 415-776
7825 ⓦ BART Powell St
ⓦ Muni 2, 3, 4 ◷
lunch 11.30am-2pm,
dinner 5.30-10pm; bar
menu till midnight ⚲ OK

Stars   SSS-SSSS
American
Chef Jeremiah Tower
presides over one of San
Francisco's long-standing
'greats'. Cocktails and
wine are given great
attention, and an inexpensive bar menu is perfect
for pre-opera dining;
there's live piano most
nights.
✉ 555 Golden Gate
Ave, Civic Center (7,
F4) ☎ 415-861 7827
ⓦ BART Civic Center
ⓦ Muni 26 ◷ 11am-
10.30pm (Fri-Sat till
11pm) ⚲ OK V

MARIN COUNTY
(5, B2)
Guaymas   SS-SSS
*Mexican/American
Southwest*
A festive Mexican-style
restaurant with creative
appetisers, an interesting
tequila/margarita menu
and patio tables overlooking San Francisco Bay. It's a
great destination and the
perfect excuse to ferry
across the Bay.
✉ 5 Main St, Tiburon
☎ 415-435 6300 ⓦ
Golden Gate Transit 10

🚢 Blue & Gold Fleet
to/from SF's Pier 39 ◷
Mon-Thurs 11.30am-
10pm, Fri-Sat 11.30am-
11pm, Sun 10.30am-
10pm V

La Ginestra   SS
Italian
No-nonsense Italian food
has been served by the
Aversa family for several
decades. Try the linguini
with clams and be sure to
save room for the home-
made tiramisu.
✉ 127 Throckmorton
Ave, Mill Valley ☎
415-388 0224 ⓦ
Golden Gate Transit 10
◷ Tues-Sun 4-10.30pm
⚲ OK

NORTH OF
DOWNTOWN
Caffé Macaroni   SS
Italian
Exceedingly intimate and
very Italian, this tiny place
has superb and authentic
food, service and atmos-
phere. Sit upstairs if you
can.
✉ 59 Columbus Ave,
North Beach (7, C3) ☎
415-956 9737 ⓦ BART
Montgomery ◷ Mon-
Sat 5-10pm ⚲ OK V

Greens   SSS
Vegetarian
Arguably the city's best-
known vegetarian restau-
rant, this elegant spot has
an unbeatable vantage
point from which to watch
the sun sink below the
Golden Gate Bridge.
✉ Bldg A, Fort Mason
Center, The Marina (6,
E1) ☎ 415-771 6222
ⓦ Muni 28 ◷ lunch
Tues-Fri 11.30am-2pm,
Sat 11.30am-2.30pm,
Sun 10am-2pm; dinner
nightly 5.30-9.30pm
(Fri till 10pm) ⚲ OK

L'Osteria del Forno $$
Italian

It's a tiny neighbourhood place run by a couple of no-nonsense Italian women who make wonderful hand-made ravioli and pizza. First dates, marriage proposals, divorces and impromptu occasions all happen here. The menu is basic, but nightly specials are 'outta dis woyld'.

✉ 519 Columbus Ave, North Beach (7, C2) ☎ 415-982 1124 🚌 Muni 30 🕐 Wed-Mon 11.30am-10pm V

Swan Oyster Depot

Simon Bracken

Mama's on Washington Square $
American

Big hearty American breakfasts including eggs any which way, banana and nut French toast, buttermilk pancakes and a huge range of sandwiches.

✉ cnr Stockton & Filbert Sts, North Beach (7, C2) ☎ 415-362 6421 🚌 Muni 15 🕐 8am-3pm V

Mario's Bohemian Cigar Store $-$$
Italian

An unquestionable North Beach tradition, this inexpensive cafe/bar/restaurant looks out onto Washington Square and has great focaccia.

✉ 566 Columbus Ave, North Beach (7, C2) ☎ 415-362 0536 🚌 Muni 30 🚋 Powell-Mason cable car 🕐 10am-midnight (Sun to 11pm)

Osome $$$
Japanese

A large menu focused on sushi and sashimi, traditional seating and artistic presentation make this a good choice for high-end Japanese food. It's in a pretty, relatively

quiet, part of town that's good for strolling.

✉ 3145 Fillmore St, Cow Hollow (6, F1) ☎ 415-931 8898 🚌 Muni 30, 45 🕐 5.30-11pm

Swan Oyster Depot $
Seafood

Belly up to the bar at this 80-year-old San Fran institution where fresh oysters and an unbridled ambience are the key attractions.

✉ 1517 Polk St, Nob Hill (7, E2) ☎ 415-673 1101 🚌 Muni 19 to California St 🕐 8am-5.30pm

SOUTH OF DOWNTOWN
Cha Cha Cha $$
Caribbean/Spanish

A crowded, colourful place with excellent Caribbean-influenced tapas. The wait for a table can be extraordinarily long, but the people-watching and fine sangria help make it enjoyable.

✉ 1801 Haight St, Upper Haight (7, J2) ☎ 415-386 7670 🕐 3.30-11pm V

Fringale $$-$$$
French

Long known as one of SF's best, this popular Basque-inspired French bistro is surprisingly good value. Specialities include fish stew, rack of lamb and a wonderful array of desserts.

✉ 570 4th St, SoMa (6, C3) ☎ 415-543 0573 🚇 BART Powell St 🕐 lunch Mon-Fri 11.30am-3pm, dinner Mon-Sat 5.30-10.30pm ♿ no

Hamburger Mary's $-$$
American Fast Food
One of the city's all-time

Taquerías

Though there's a shortage of quality Mexican restaurants in San Francisco (especially compared with LA), the city makes up for it with an abundance of *taquerías*. Taquerías have cafeteria assembly-line service and specialise in simple fare such as tacos and burritos. Food is commonly wrapped in aluminium foil, even if you plan to eat in.

The beauty of the taquerías is that you rarely have to spend more than $5 for a San Francisco-style burrito (packed with rice, beans, grilled meat, salsa, guacamole and sour cream) or soft tacos washed down with a Mexican beer or *agua fresca* (fresh fruit punch).

ate-night hang-outs, where colourful characters chow large, tasty burgers amidst authentic junk shop clutter. The heavily-pierced staff is exceedingly friendly. ⊠ cnr Folsom & 12th Sts, SoMa (7, F5) ☎ 415-626 1985 🚌 Muni 9 ⏱ Tues-Sun 11.30am-midnight ♿ kids' menu **V**

India Oven   **$$**
Indian

Good prices, great garlic *naan* and authentically Indian service in a lively setting. BYOB for the line that forms on Friday and Saturday nights! ⊠ 233 Fillmore St, Lower Haight (7, G4) ☎ 415-626 1628 🚇 BART Powell St ⏱ lunch 11.30am-2pm, dinner 5.30-9.30pm (Fri-Sat to 10.30pm) **V**

Sleek and funky LuLu

You Want a What!!??
The American taste for cocktails originated during Prohibition, when flavoursome mixers were used to disguise the taste of bathtub gin. These days there are thousands of cocktail recipes, and many bars have their own concoctions, usually with a humorous name, like the Screaming Orgasm or the Slippery Nipple.

La Méditerranée   **$$**
Middle Eastern

Small and comfortable, this place serves reliably good Middle Eastern eats. Try the sample plate of hummus, tabouli, baba ghanoush and dolmas or the chicken celicia (filo-wrapped, spiced with cinnamon and raisins). ⊠ 288 Noe St, The Castro (7, H4) ☎ 415-431 210 🚇 Muni F, K, L, M ⏱ 11am-10pm (Fri till 11pm) **V**

LuLu   **$$$-$$$$**
Californian

This modern, spacious restaurant tops the hip list. Cal-Mediterranean dishes come from the exposed kitchen, sleek and funky cocktails from the bar. Order a number of small plates and share – it's the thing to do. ⊠ 816 Folsom St, SoMa (7, D5) ☎ 415-495 5775 🚇 BART Powell St ⏱ lunch 11.30am-3pm, dinner 5.30-10.30pm (Fri to 11.30pm) ♿ OK **V**

Pancho Villa Taquería   **$**
Mexican

If there's a definitive Mission taquería, this is it. Wrap yourself around a carnitas, tofu or shrimp burrito if you're bored with chicken and beef. The line moves quickly, so don't be disheartened if it's out the door when you arrive. ⊠ 3071 16th St, The Mission (7, G5) ☎ 415-864 8840 🚇 BART 16th & Mission ⏱ 10am-midnight **V**

Slanted Door   **$$-$$$**
Vietnamese/Californian

California-influenced Vietnamese food served with such artistic flare that taste could become secondary – but it doesn't. The ambience is cool and trendy and the clientele defines hip. ⊠ 584 Valencia St, The Mission (7, G5) ☎ 415-861 8032 🚇 BART 16th & Mission ⏱ Tues-Sun lunch 11.30am-3pm, dinner 5-10pm

Thep Phanom   **$-$$**
Thai

Consistently rated the best Thai eatery in San Francisco, with refined food and service to match. ⊠ 400 Waller St, Lower Haight (7, G4) ☎ 415-431 2526 🚌 Muni 32, 47 ⏱ 5.30-10.30pm **V**

iquor Talk
l bars have a big range of 'hard liquor' – gin, randy, rum, vodka, whiskey – invariably served with ts of ice ('on the rocks') unless you ask for it traight up'. If you ask for whiskey you'll get merican whiskey (sometimes called bourbon). If ou want Scotch whiskey, ask for Scotch.

SAN DIEGO

San Diego's hippest and most diner-friendly neighbourhoods (the Gaslamp Quarter, Hillcrest, La Jolla) tend to have mostly seafood, Mexican and Italian. The Gaslamp Quarter has more than 65 restaurants offering everything from fast gourmet to multi-course Indian. Kids like Horton Plaza (9, E3) rooftop food court. Places along the beach offer inexpensive food; Garnet Ave, Pacific Beach (8, D2), is especially good for pub grub.

DOWNTOWN

Dakota Grill & Spirits $$-$$$

Californian/Southwest
Casual, fun and oh-so-hip, the first-rate cuisine is matched by home-brewed beer and a big wine list. Watch the chef grill chicken and steaks, slide pizzas out of the wood-fired oven, and toss salads galore.
✉ 901 5th Ave, Gaslamp Quarter (9, D4) ☎ 619-234 5554 🚍 MTS 1, 3, 5, 16, 25 🚇 to 5th Ave ⏰ lunch Mon-Fri 11.30am-2.30pm, dinner Mon-Thurs 5-10pm, Fri-Sat 5-11pm, Sun 5-9pm ♿ no Ⓥ

Fio's Cucina Italiana $$-$$$

Italian
Pricey but not outrageous, this is one of the Gaslamp Quarter's consistent bests.

Cheap Eats

Tuesday is a good night to eat in the **Hillcrest** district (8, F4). Most places on and around University and Fifth Aves have Tuesday night specials that range from a free appetiser to buy-one-get-one-free meals. Go early (around 5pm) and choose from places displaying the Tuesday Night Out sticker.

Elegant decor, live piano on weekends and a long wine list complement the inventive Italian fare.
✉ 801 5th Ave, Gaslamp Quarter (9, D4) ☎ 619-234 3467 🚍 MTS 1, 3, 5, 16, 25 🚇 to 5th Ave ⏰ Sun-Thurs 5pm-midnight, Fri-Sat 5pm-1am ♿ not great Ⓥ

The Fish Market $$-$$$

Seafood
An extensive menu featuring grilled salmon, fresh (or baked or fried) oysters, sushi and other seafood delights. The ambience is energetic, casual but classy and the view of the harbour is good from every table. Upstairs, at **Top O' the Market**, prices are double.
✉ Tuna La, Downtown (9, E1) ☎ 619-232 3474 🚍 MTS 7, 20, 40, 70, 210, 850, 860 🚇 Seaport Village ⏰ 11am-10pm ♿ OK; kid's menu Ⓥ

Mimmo's Italian Village $

Italian Deli
Fresh ingredients and plenty of herbs and spices make the salads (and there's a lot of them) outstanding and the hot meatball sandwiches memorable. Pizza and pasta are also available.
✉ 1743 India St, Little Italy (9, B2) ☎ 619-239 3710 🚍 MTS 5, 16 🚇 Blue Line to County

Center/Little Italy ⏰ 8am-6pm ♿ excellent Ⓥ

Mr A's Restaurant $$$-$$$$

American
This ultimate old-school, upscale restaurant has panoramic views of the city and bay. The menu is unswervingly traditional – chateaubriand, rack of lamb, baked Alaska – and the martinis are as authentic as they come.
✉ 2250 5th Ave, Downtown (9, D4) ☎ 619-239 1377 🚍 MTS 1, 3, 5, 16, 25 ⏰ lunch Mon-Fri 11am-2.30pm, dinner 5.30-10pm ♿ ye

Royal Thai $$-$$$

Thai
The chef here is not bashful when concocting curries. The menu features traditional Thai dishes – infused with garlic, basil, lemongrass, chilli – served in healthy proportions. Large, colourful art pieces deck the walls and Thai music tinkles beneath the hum of happy diners.
✉ 467 5th Ave, Gaslamp Quarter (9, E4) ☎ 619-230 8424 🚍 MTS 1, 3, 5, 16, 25 🚇 to 5th Ave ⏰ lunch daily 11am-3pm, dinner Sun-Thurs 5-10pm, Fri-Sat 5pm-midnight ♿ OK Ⓥ

LA JOLLA

Bahia Don Bravo $

Mexican
From the carne asada

supreme to the low-fat black bean vegie, the burritos here are big and tasty – and the chicken tamales and lobster enchiladas are just as good.

✉ 5504 La Jolla Blvd (8, D1) ☎ 858-454 8940 🚍 MTS 34, 34A ⊙ 7am-10pm ♿ yes

Brockton Villa $-$$
American

In a refurbished California bungalow perched above La Jolla Cove, this place has good breakfasts, fresh seafood and outstanding coffee. Sit outside (if the pelican poop smell is not too bad) or inside among the historic photos and rugs.

✉ 1235 Coast Blvd, La Jolla (8, C1) ☎ 858-454 7393 🚍 MTS 34, 34A ⊙ daily 8am-3pm, dinner Tues-Sun 5-9pm ♿ OK for breakfast or lunch

The Marine Room $$$
Seafood/Californian

In winter the waves splash the windows of this La Jolla institution, whose menu is inventive and presentation impeccable. Seafood prepared to reflect the season and eclectic desserts are specialties. Come for fish tacos at the bar if you're on the run.

✉ 2000 Spindrift Dr, La Jolla Shores (8, C1) ☎ 858-459 7222 🚍 MTS 30, 34, 34A, 34B ⊙ lunch 11.30am-2.30pm, dinner 6-10pm ♿ no **V**

NORTH OF DOWNTOWN

Mission Hills Cafe $$
Californian/French

With white linen and fresh flowers on each table, this local favourite offers San Diego's best fixed-price menu. There's rustic soups, salads and grilled specialties with a provincial French flare; à la carte items also available.

✉ 808 W Washington St, Mission Hills (8, F4) ☎ 619-296 8010 🚍 MTS 3, 8, 16, 990 ⊙ 8am-4pm (breakfast till 3pm) & 5-10pm ♿ OK **V**

Old Town Mexican Cafe $$
Mexican

Best among the Old Town eateries for home-made tortillas, seafood enchiladas and *machacas* (shredded pork with onions and peppers).

✉ 2489 San Diego Ave, Old Town (8, F3) ☎ 619-297 4330 🚍 MTS to Old Town 🚉 Old Town Transit Center ⊙ 7am-11pm,

Fri-Sat 7am-midnight ♿ good kids menu

Thai Foon $-$$$
Thai

Arguably the best of Hillcrest's Thai restaurants, this friendly little place is refined yet casual and extremely comfortable. Stand-out dishes include excellent yellow curries and green papaya salad.

✉ 540 University Ave, Hillcrest (8, F4) ☎ 619-297 8424 🚍 MTS 8, 11, 16, 990 ⊙ lunch Mon-Sat 11am-3pm, dinner daily 5-11pm ♿ yes **V**

PACIFIC & MISSION BEACHES

The Mission Cafe $-$$
Californian

A hip place for casual, healthy meals with an emphasis on vegetarian cooking. Black beans, fresh salsa and polenta appear in many dishes, from breakfast frittatas to lunch roll-ups and salads. Just as good are the home-made pastries and coffee.

✉ 3795 Mission Blvd, Mission Beach (8, E1) ☎ 858-488 9060 🚍 MTS 27, 34, 34A, 34B ⊙ Mon-Fri 7am-3pm, Sat-Sun 7am-4pm ♿ OK **V**

World Famous $$
American

The dining room is as casual as the boardwalk-side patio, and every seat has an ocean view. The fish tacos are easily among San Diego's best; prime rib and burgers are also popular, as are bar menu items like cheese-filled potato skins and fried shrimp.

✉ 711 Pacific Beach Dr, Pacific Beach (8, E1) ☎ 858-272 3100 🚍 MTS 27, 34, 34A, 34B ⊙ 7am-11pm (bar till 1am) ♿ kid's menu

ate Night Snacks

ie Pannikin, 7467 Girard Ave, La Jolla (8, C1), for ood Java coffee and a sunny patio

ie Living Room, 1010 Prospect St, La Jolla (8, C1), as gorgeous cakes and light meals until midnight

elato Verro Caffe, cnr Washington & India Sts (8, F4), a late-night hangout with superb Italian ice cream

afe LuLu, 419 F St, Gaslamp Quarter (9, E4), is very ic, with pastries and light meals till 4am

avid's Place, 3766 5th Ave, Hillcrest (8, F4), brews e best espresso and is the city's gay hub

AROUND CALIFORNIA

BIG SUR (1, G4)
Nepenthe & Cafe
Kevah $-$$$
Californian/American
Known for its elaborate gardens, sprawling cliffside location and eccentric owners, Nepenthe uses local produce, fresh herbs, game and seafood. Just below the main restaurant, **Cafe Kevah** has salads, soups and sandwiches.
✉ **Hwy 1, 29 miles south of Carmel** ☎ **831-667 2345** ⏱ **lunch 11.30am-4.30pm, dinner 5-10pm** ♿ **yes** **V**

Village Pub $-$$
Pub Grub
With wonderful soups, fish & chips and vegie burgers, it's also one of the least pretentious places in the area.
✉ **Hwy 1, next to the River Inn Resort** ☎ **831-667 2355** ⏱ **June-Sept 12-9pm; Oct-May: Thurs-Tues 3-8.30pm**

Ventana Big Sur $$$
Californian
A romantically rustic restaurant with impeccable service, artistic and tasty dishes and a stunning wine list. Cosy fine dining does

not get much better.
✉ **Hwy 1, next to the River Inn Resort** ☎ **831-667 2331** ⏱ **lunch 12-3pm, dinner 6-9pm** ♿ **no**

EUREKA (1, B2)
Hotel Carter $$-$$$
Californian/American
A gourmet restaurant that has won many awards for excellence; it's famous both for its breakfasts (a 4-course meal and lavish buffet) and its gourmet dinners (with 30-page wine list).
✉ **301 L St at 3rd St** ☎ **707-444 8062** 🚌 **HTA to Old Town Eureka** ⏱ **breakfast 7.30-10am, dinner 6-9pm** ♿ **OK** **V**

Samoa
Cookhouse $-$$
Rustic American
Eureka's best-known eatery, this 1893 lumberjack cookhouse is a slice out of the past. Diners are seated all together, then served 'all-you-can-eat' courses of hearty dishes. Dinner includes soup, salad, meats, vegetables, apple pie and hot drinks; breakfast and lunch are similarly filling. There's also a museum on site.

✉ **Samoa Rd, Eureka** ☎ **707-442 1659** ⏱ **Mon-Sat 6am-3.30pm & 5-9pm, Sun 6am-9pm** ♿ **yes**

GOLD COUNTRY (1, D4)
Tofanelli's $
American
Well-known for its friendly service, simple atmosphere and reliably good food (especially breakfast and baked goods). Burgers – beef, vegie or turkey – and the apple cobbler are consistent winners.
✉ **302 W Main St, Grass Valley** ☎ **530-272 1468** 🚌 **Gold Country Stage from Nevada City** ⏱ **daily 7am-3pm, Fri-Sun 5-9pm** ♿ **kids' menu**

Old Nevada
Brewery $-$$
Italian
In the town's original brewery, it produces top-notch ales, lagers and porters. Light meals are served in the lively brew-pub, while the upstairs restaurant has pasta, large salads and grilled meats and fish.
✉ **107 Sacramento St, Nevada City** ☎ **530-**

Fast Food
Many fast food chains are characteristically Californian – efficient, convenient, colourful and close to the freeway. Die-hard fast foodies will travel 50 miles for an In-N-Out burger, said to be the best of the bunch; the others are McDonald's, Burger King, Carl's Jnr and Wendy's. Jack-in-the-Box and Taco Bell have quasi-Mexican food.

Pizza Hut, Shakey's, Straw Hat and Round Table do pizza; they often have video games and other amusements for kids. California Pizza Kitchen, usually found in malls, offers a more gourmet spin.

Johnny Rockets – one of dozens of chains offering fast food

265 3960 ☺ lunch
11am-2pm, dinner 5-
9pm (Fri-Sat to 10pm)
♿ kids' menu

Zinfandel's $$-$$$
Californian
Said to be the finest
restaurant in the Gold
Country, famous for its
eclectic Californian menu
and superb wine list.
The house it's in is in a refurbished relic, complete with
slanting floors and a porch.
✉ cnr Main & Hanford
Sts, Sutter Creek ☎ 209-
267 5008 ☺ Thurs-Sun
5.30pm-late ♿ yes **V**

MENDOCINO (1, D2)
Cafe Beaujolais $$$
French/Californian
Mendocino's, and possibly
Northern California's, most
famous restaurant, 'cafe
booge' draws diners from
all parts of the Bay Area.
The ambience is rustic and
charming, the food innovative and hearty.
✉ 961 Ukiah St ☎
707-937 5614 ☺ 5.45-
9pm ♿ OK

MONTEREY
PENINSULA (1, F4)
Forge in the
Forest $$-$$$
American
Dine on the flower-filled patio
or in the rustic interior where
there's an authentic blacksmith's forge. The California-
influenced classic-American
food has won several awards,
and there's a daily happy
hour with free appetisers.
✉ cnr 5th & Junipero
Sts, Carmel ☎ 831-624
2233 ☺ 11.30am-
10pm (Fri-Sat to 11pm),
bar open till 1am ♿
kids' menu **V**

Fresh Cream $$$$
European/American

Serves up delicious European
dishes with a picture-window
view of the wharf. This place
deserves its bundle of culinary awards; try the lobster
ravioli or rack of lamb, and
anything the sommelier recommends will be excellent.
✉ Heritage Harbor com-
plex, Fisherman's Wharf,
Monterey ☎ 831-375
9798 ☺ restaurant: 6-
10pm; bar: 5pm-late ♿
early evening best

Old Monterey
Café $-$$
American
Resolutely old-fashioned,
with plate-warping breakfasts
(served all day), sandwiches
and some Mexican dishes.
✉ 489 Alvarado St,
Monterey ☎ 831-646
1021 ☺ Wed-Mon
7am-2.30pm ♿ yes **V**

Tarpy's
Roadhouse $$$
American
In rustic 1917 digs, this place
garners accolades for its
comfort and retro-American
food. Corn and potatoes play
big roles on the menu, and
the pork chops are to die for.
✉ 2999 Monterey/
Salinas Hwy 1, at Hwy
68 & Canyon Del Rey
☎ 831-647 1444 ☺
11.30am-10pm ♿ OK **V**

PALM SPRINGS
(1, J8)
Las Casuelas $$
Mexican

A local favourite for more
than 40 years. The servings
are generous, the margaritas have a good kick and
the setting is surprisingly
tropical for the middle of
the desert.
✉ 368 N Palm Canyon
Dr ☎ 760-325 3213 🚌
Greyhound from LA &
San Diego ☺ 10am-
10pm (Fri-Sat till 11pm)
♿ kids' serves **V**

Louise's Pantry $-$$
American
Distinctly American diner
that's been *the* spot for
breakfast for years. The
food hasn't changed much,
but it's fine if you're happy
to skip espresso coffee and
designer pancakes.
✉ 44491 Town Center
Way, Palm Desert ☎
760-346 9320 ☺ 7am-
8pm ♿ kids' menu

SACRAMENTO
(1, D4)
California Fats $$-$$$
Pacific Rim
Most items have a Cal-Asian
twist, telling of the Chinese
heritage of the Fat family.
Rock shrimp pasta and pot-
stickers (steamed dumplings)
with dipping sauces are
house specialties. The colour
scheme accentuates the 2-
storey glass waterfall.
✉ 1015 Front St ☎
916-441 7966 🚌
Downtown Area Shuttle
☺ lunch Mon-Fri
11.30am-4pm, dinner

Picnicking
California's climate is very conducive to picnicking, and
you'll find many delis, markets and cafes stock all the necessary items, from pre-made salads to single-serve bottles
of wine. Health food stores and natural food markets
usually have organic produce, bulk food and a deli section with sandwiches, burritos and beverages.

Mon-Sat 5-10pm, Sun 4-9pm ♿ kids' menu

SAN LUIS OBISPO (1, G5)
SLO Brewing Co $-$$
Pub Grub
Good vegie burgers, grilled meats and fish, and large salads. The atmosphere is loud and the home-made brews are worth sampling.
✉ 1119 Garden St ☎ 805-543 1843 🚍 SLO Transit 4, 5, 6 ⏰ Mon-Wed 11.30am-10pm, Thurs-Sat 11.30am-late, Sun 11.30am-9pm ♿ kids' menu **V**

SANTA BARBARA (1, H5)
La Tolteca $
Mexican
A true no-frills 'mexi-catessen', famous for its enchiladas and tamales. There's a few small, un-atmospheric tables, but most people take food to go. Don't miss the home-made *agua fresca* (fresh fruit drinks); the *horchata* (a milky blend of rice water, sugar and cinnamon) is particularly good.
✉ 614 E Haley St ☎ 805-963 0847 🚋 trolley to cnr Haley & State Sts ⏰ 8am-8pm ♿ yes

Brophy Brothers $$
Seafood
A lively restaurant and oyster bar where locals go for reliably excellent seafood; top choices include clam chowder and *cioppino*

(seafood stew). Sunday brunch is a popular time to watch the boat traffic and drink Bloody Marys.
✉ Santa Barbara Yacht Harbor ☎ 805-966 4418 🚋 trolley to yacht harbour ⏰ 11am-10pm (Fri-Sat to 11pm) ♿ yes

SANTA CRUZ (5, F4)
Zachary's $
Californian
Inexpensive, hearty breakfasts and lunches attract all walks of life to this simple, no-risk eatery.
✉ 819 Pacific Ave ☎ 831-427 0646 ⏰ 7am-2.30pm 🚍 SCMTD 1 to 12 ♿ yes; ½ serves available **V**

Gabriella Cafe $$
Italian/Seafood
A tranquil candlelit restaurant whose menu features pasta, seafood and numerous local wines.
✉ 910 Cedar St ☎ 831-457 1677 🚍 SCMTD 1 to 12 ⏰ around 11am-10pm ♿ yes; small serves available **V**

WINE COUNTRY
Cafe at the Winery $$$
French
A favourite with locals celebrating an occasion and with Wine Country visitors. Its rustic French cuisine and view overlooking the Chateau Souverain vineyards make it a pleasure.
✉ Château Souverain winery, 400 Souverain

Rd, Geyserville (1, D3) ☎ 707-433 3141 🚍 5min drive north of Healdsburg; exit at Independence Lane from US 101 ⏰ lunch daily 11.30am-2.30pm, dinner Fri-Sun 5.30-8.30pm ♿ OK

Auberge de Soleil $$$
Californian
The views, decor and attention to detail make this a quintessential Wine Country dining experience. Try anything grilled over the vine-fed fire and ask for recommendations when choosing wine – you'll be surprised at what they come up with.
✉ 180 Rutherford Hill Rd, Rutherford (5, A3) ☎ 707-963 1211 ⏰ Mon-Fri 6-9.30pm, Sat-Sun 5.30-9.30pm ♿ no **V**

Foothill Cafe $$
American
Tucked into the most unlikely of settings – the J&P Shopping Center – it offers old fashioned barbecue and casual respite from the glamour of other Napa attractions.
✉ 2766 Old Sonoma Rd, Napa (5, A3) ☎ 707-252 6178 ⏰ Wed-Sun 4.30-9.30pm ♿ great

Tra Vigne $-$$$
Northern Italian
A stylish Tuscan-influenced Italian restaurant with a reputation for some of the best food in the Napa Valley. In the walled garden patio is a deli and wine shop that serves quicker, less-expensive meals and gourmet picnic supplies.
✉ 1050 Charter Oak Ave, St Helena (1, D3) ☎ 707-963 4444 ⏰ 11.30am-10.30pm (Oct-May till 10pm)

Once hectic, noisy and smelly, Cannery Row is now a tourist precinct of restaurants and shops.

entertainment

California's main cities offer a mind-boggling array of entertainment options – everything from opera to professional football. LA is the undisputed theatre capital, and nearby San Diego also has an excellent thespian scene. San Francisco and LA both have outstanding symphony orchestras, while Oakland is the place for jazz and blues. The university town of Berkeley is home to one of the most influential punk clubs ever.

Cinema is obviously huge in LA, but the San Francisco Bay Area is also cinematically abuzz with its wonderful old cinemas, discerning local film buffs and lots of foreign and arthouse venues. Smaller Californian towns usually have at least one venue (pub, lounge, cantina, brewery) for live music on weekends, plus a movie theatre.

Big-name performers usually follow the same California route: the San Diego Sports Arena; LA's Staples Center, Hollywood Bowl or Greek Theater; and San Francisco Peninsula's Shoreline Theater or Oakland's Coliseum.

What's Hot Where

Theatre – LA & San Diego
Comedy – LA
Dance – San Francisco
Blues & Jazz – Oakland, LA
Classical Music – LA & San Francisco
Rap & Hip-Hop – LA
Cinema – LA & San Francisco

In the Know

Weekly publications – *LA Weekly*, *SF Weekly* and the *San Diego Reader* – and the entertainment section of local newspapers are the best source of up-to-date information on all types of entertainment.

Just the Ticket

Tickets for most big-name shows and professional sports events are sold through ticketing agencies, which charge a $3 booking fee per ticket. Try Ticketmaster in LA (☎ 213-381 2000) and San Diego (☎ 619-268 8526), BASS in the San Francisco Bay Area (☎ 510-762 2277). These agencies also have outlets in Wherehouse, Tower Records, Robinson's-May and Macy's stores.

Half-price tickets are usually sold on the day of a performance (or day before for matinees). In LA get them from Times Tix at Jerry's Famous Deli (☎ 310-659 3678; Thurs-Sun 12-6pm), 8701 Beverly Blvd (4, F2). In San Francisco try TIX Bay Area (☎ 415-433 7827; Tues-Thurs 11am-6pm, Fri-Sat 11am-7pm), 251 Stockton St, Union Square (7, D4). In San Diego it's Times Arts Tix (☎ 619-497 5000), on Broadway, opposite Horton Plaza (9, D4).

All made up for the Chinese New Year

Rush Tickets

Many theatres offer 'rush' tickets – unsold tickets sold cheaper just before the performance. There are no reservations or guarantees on these tickets, and they are sometimes limited to students and seniors.

What's On

The *Golden California Special Events* booklet has a complete list of the state's events. To get one, contact the California Division of Tourism (☎ 800-862 2543), PO Box 1499, Sacramento.

January *Tournament of Roses* – 1 Jan; Rose Bowl Parade & Rose Bowl football game, Pasadena, LA
Chinese New Year – Jan-Feb; biggest celebrations are in SF and LA
San Diego Marathon – 2nd weekend

February *African-American Cultural Heritage Parade & Expo* – Oakland
Pacific Orchid Exposition – last week; San Francisco

March *Academy Awards ceremony* – LA
Snowfest – last weekend; winter carnival held in Truckee and around Lake Tahoe
Redwood Coast Dixieland Jazz Festival – last weekend; Eureka

April *Long Beach Grand Prix* – 2nd weekend; LA
Cherry Blossom Festival – 2nd weekend; SF
San Francisco International Film Festival – last weekend to 1st weekend of May
I Madonnari Italian Street Painting Festival – San Luis Obispo

May *Bay to Breakers run* – SF
Carnaval – last weekend; pre-Lent party with music and dancing in The Mission, SF

June *Indian Fair* – 3rd weekend; San Diego
Gay Freedom Day Parade – SF
Christopher St West Gay & Lesbian Pride Festival – West Hollywood
Playboy Jazz Festival – 2nd & 3rd weekend; Hollywood Bowl, LA
Mariachi USA Festival – LA

July *4th of July* – US Independence Day; celebrations statewide
Catalina Dixieland Jazz Fest – Avalon, Santa Catalina Island
US Open Surfing Competition – 3rd weekend; Huntington Beach, LA
US Open Sandcastle Contest – 3rd weekend; Imperial Beach, San Diego
Laguna Arts Festival – see page 98

August *Old Spanish Days Fiesta* – Santa Barbara
Nisei Week Japanese Festival – LA
African Marketplace & Cultural Fair – LA
Long Beach Jazz Festival – 2nd weekend; LA

September *Monterey Grand Prix*
Shakespeare Festival – SF; free performances in various parks
San Diego Street Scene – Gaslamp Quarter
Monterey Jazz Festival – mid-month
Watts Towers Jazz Festival – LA
Oktoberfest – Sept-Oct; statewide

October *Halloween* – statewide; especially wild in The Castro (SF) and West Hollywood

November *Thanksgiving* – 4th Thursday; traditionally celebrated with big family dinner, usually turkey and autumn harvest vegetables

December *New Year's Eve* – riotous parties statewide

LOS ANGELES

THEATRE & COMEDY

Comedy & Magic Club

Jay Leno plays most Sundays and Billy Crystal has been known to drop in at this nightclub-by-the-beach that's hosted quality comedy and magic acts for more than 20 years. Bookings required Friday and Saturday, recommended on Sunday.
✉ **1018 Hermosa Ave, Hermosa Beach (2, F2) ☎ 310-372 1193 [e] www.comedyandmagicclub.com 🚌 MTA 439 🕘 box office Tues-Sat 12.30-9pm, Sun 12.30-8pm; performances Tues-Fri 8pm, Sat 5.30 & 9pm, Sun 7pm 👪 over 18s only**

Comedy Store

The hottest of LA's comedy clubs has 3 stages and a range of styles – from sketch to improv to stand-up. Performers include the well-known and the unknown.
✉ **8433 Sunset Blvd, W Hollywood (4, F1) ☎ 323-656 6225 [e] www.comedystore.com 🚌 MTA 2, 3 🕘 8pm-1am $ $8-$15; 2-drink minimum 👪 over 21s only**

Groundling Theater

A repertory company whose alumni include Peewee Herman, the late Phil Hartman and Julia Sweeney.
✉ **7307 Melrose Ave, W Hollywood (4, D3) ☎ 323-934 9700 [e] www.groundlings.com 🚌 MTA 10 🕘 shows Thurs 8pm, Fri-Sat 8 & 10pm, Sun 7.30pm $ $10-$17.50 👪 parental guidance suggested for ages 17 and under**

The Improv

Some shows are better than others but it's always packed; a very lively bar scene.
✉ **8162 Melrose Ave, W Hollywood (4, D3) ☎ 323-651 2583 [e] www.improvclub.com 🚌 MTA 10, 11 🕘 Mon-Thurs 8pm, Fri-Sat 8.30 & 10.30pm $ $8-$11 👪 over 16s only**

Matrix Theater

If it were anywhere else but LA (or maybe New York), this would be *the* pinnacle of off-Broadway productions. Drama, satire and the occasional mystery is on offer.
✉ **7657 Melrose Ave, W Hollywood (4, D3) ☎ 323-852 1445 🚌 MTA 10, 11 🕘 box office: noon to curtain**

Music Center of LA County (3, E2)

The centre is the collective name for the Dorothy Chandler Pavilion (home to the LA Philharmonic), the Ahmanson Theater (musicals and plays from Broadway) and the Mark Taper Forum (experimental drama, US and world premieres).
✉ **135 N Grand Ave, Downtown ☎ 213-972 7211 🚌 DASH A, B 🕘 box office Mon-Fri 9am-5pm & 2hrs before show $ varies; rush tickets $8-$20**

Shubert Theater

(4, K3) This is where the big-time musical productions such as *Cats*, *Phantom of the Opera* and *Sunset Boulevard* show in LA.
✉ **2020 Avenue of the Stars, Century City ☎ 310-201 1555 (theatre), 800-233 3123 (sales) [e] www.telecharge.com 🚌 MTA 4 🕘 Mon-Wed & Fri-Sat 10am-5pm, Thurs 10am-8pm, Sun 11am-3pm $ senior & student rush tickets available**

Wadsworth Theater

Harbours the UCLA Center for the Performing Arts' prolific program of self-produced and guest musical and dance performances, including the Jazz Philharmonic.
✉ **10920 Wilshire Blvd, Westwood (2, C1) ☎ 310-825 2101 [e] www.pto.ucla.edu 🚌 MTA 20 🕘 box office Mon-Fri 9am-5pm &**

David Peevers

Lipschitz Fountain, in the forecourt of the Music Center of LA County

1hr before show times $ possible rush tickets half an hour before perfomances

BARS, PUBS & LOUNGES

Aloha Sharkeez

Taking honours for the longest line and loudest decor on Hermosa Beach's lively Pier Ave Plaza scene, this place serves mysterious concoctions like Lava Flow and Blue Voodoo in 48oz pitchers and 80oz buckets. Luckily there are plenty of taxis around at the end of the night.
✉ 52 Pier Ave, Hermosa Beach (2, F2) ☎ 310-374 7823 🚌 MTA 130, 439 🕘 5pm-2am

Cat & Fiddle

An English-style pub with darts, snooker and a good selection of beers on tap.
✉ 6530 Sunset Blvd, Hollywood (4, B2) ☎ 323-468 3800 🚌 MTA 2, 3 🕘 11.30am-2am

Dresden Room

An LA institution since the 1950s, it made a comeback after being featured in the film *Swingers*. The camp singing duo of Marty & Elaine accompany the ever-present piano; they pack in an inter-generational crowd of hipsters.
✉ 1760 N Vermont Ave, Los Feliz (2, B4) ☎ 323-665 4294 🚌 MTA 1, 180, 181, 206, 217 🕘 Mon-Sat 9pm-1.15am

O2 Bar

Only in LA will you find a place that serves elixirs, smoothies and a variety of oxygen supplements while trance and dance music, acoustic folk and world fusion titillate your senses.
✉ cnr Sunset Blvd & Holloway Dr, W Hollywood (4, F1) ☎ 310-360 9002 🚌 MTA 2, 3, 105, 302, 429 🕘 Tues-Sat 9pm-late

MUSIC & DANCE CLUBS

Catalina Bar & Grill

LA's top jazz venue draws big-name musicians from around the world. All ages are welcome; smart dress required.
✉ 1640 N Cahuenga Blvd, Hollywood (4, B2) ☎ 323-466 2210 🚌 MTA 163 🕘 shows Tues-Sat 8.30 & 10.30pm, Sun 7 & 9pm

Conga Room

A roster of celebs headed by Jimmy Smits and Jennifer Lopez co-owns this chic, super-trendy club where top-notch bands create a sizzling atmosphere. You'll find big-name Brazilian and salsa acts, jam sessions, dancing and dance lessons and 2 full bars.
✉ 5634 Wilshire Blvd, Hollywood (4, D4) ☎ 323-938 1696 🚌 MTA 20, 21, 22, 212, 320, 322 🕘 Wed-Sat; music from 10pm

Shaking his bootie at the Conga Room

The Derby

LA's 'swing central' since 1993, this place proves the swing dancing revival is here to stay. There are curtained booths for privacy-seekers and free swing lessons Sunday-Thursday at 8pm.
✉ 4500 Los Feliz Blvd, Silver Lake (2, B4) ☎ 323-663 8979 🚌 MTA 180, 181 🕘 music Sun-Tues & Thurs from 9.30pm, Fri-Sat & Wed from 10pm $ $5-$7

Dragonfly

The musical repertoire includes funk, disco, reggae and hip-hop, but it's also known as a place for moshing and slam dancing. The patio is a big attraction.
✉ 6510 Santa Monica Blvd, Hollywood (4, B3) ☎ 323-466 6111

Behind the Scenes, On the Streets

You'll often see movies, TV shows and videos being filmed on the streets of LA: traffic will be blocked by cameras, props and 18-wheel trailers bearing people, wardrobe and equipment. Stand on the sidelines and you may see a celebrity descend upon the scene, at the last minute before shooting begins. For a list of what is being filmed each day, stop by the City of LA Film & Video Permit Office, 9622 Hollywood Blvd (4, D1), 8am-5pm.

Swing at The Derby

🚌 MTA 4, 304 ⏰ music 9pm-2am

Harvelle's
Leading live blues club since 1931, Harvelle's packs people in on the weekends – come early to avoid a long queue. Beach wear not allowed.
✉ 1432 4th St, Santa Monica (2, D1) ☎ 310-395 1676 🚌 MTA 434; SM 2 ⏰ music 8.30pm-late

House of Blues
One in the ever-expanding chain, this Southern country-style venue has been around since the early 80s. It books all the big-name acts (blues, jazz, world, funk, reggae) and does a terrific Sunday gospel brunch (9.30am & 2.30pm).
✉ 8430 Sunset Blvd, W Hollywood (4, F1) ☎ 323-848 5100 🚌 MTA 2, 3, 302, 429 ⏰ music from around 8.30pm

Key Club
Two levels of high-energy club scene. Live music ranges from country to acid jazz. After the Wednesday-Sunday live shows DJs spin house, electro, hip-hop and techno till the wee hours.
✉ 9039 Sunset Blvd, W Hollywood (4, G1) ☎ 310-274 5800 🚌 MTA 2, 3, 302, 429 ⏰ music 8pm, food served till 1am 💲 $10 and up

The Lighthouse Cafe
Jazz musicians from around the world speak fondly of this ultra-casual club by the beach. It has recently been revitalised by the popularity of Hermosa Beach's Pier Ave Plaza. Weekend jazz brunch is popular, though the music is usually better than the food.
✉ 39 Pier Ave, Hermosa Beach (2, F2) ☎ 310-372 6911 🚌 MTA 130, 439 ⏰ music Tues-Thurs from 9pm, Fri from 4pm, Sat-Sun from 11am

The Roxy (4, G1)
Older favourites like Neil Young and Bruce Springsteen join the usual line-up of tomorrow's top bands at this always avant-garde club. All ages are allowed; Monday night is amateur night.
✉ 9009 Sunset Blvd, Hollywood ☎ 310-278 9457 🚌 MTA 2, 3, 302, 429 ⏰ doors open 7pm 💲 Mon $5, Tues-Sun $10-$25

Whisky a Go Go
(4, G1) A legend in Jim Morrison history and the LA music scene, it serves up a nightly feast of rock 'n' roll bands – from national headliners to up-and-coming hopefuls.
✉ 8901 Sunset Blvd, W Hollywood ☎ 310-652 4202 🚌 MTA 2, 3, 302, 429 ⏰ shows start 8pm 💲 Mon $10-$15, Tues-Thurs $10, Fri-Sun $12-$15

CLASSICAL MUSIC, DANCE & OPERA
The Greek Theater
In a natural bowl in Griffith Park, the theatre opened in 1929 and seats more than 6000 people. Year-round music headliners and ballet companies grace the stage; try to get seats close to the stage for better acoustics.
✉ 2700 N Vermont Ave, Griffith Park, Hollywood Hills (2, B4) ☎ 213-665 5857 🚌 MTA 96 ⏰ box office Mon-Fri 9am-5pm & 2hrs before show 💲 rush tickets for some performances

Hollywood Bowl
(4, B1) An outdoor amphitheatre that is the summer home of the LA Philharmonic and Hollywood Bowl Orchestra. Concert-going with a picnic and a bottle of wine has been a tradition since the

Multi Mega Movies
Cinemas – usually multiplexes with up to 20 screens – are ubiquitous in LA, the movie capital of the world. First-run films sell out early on Friday and Saturday nights. Shows after 6pm cost around $7, those before are often discounted. Credit card bookings can be made by calling ☎ 213-777 3456 or ☎ 310-777 3456, or by logging on to www.movielink.com; there's no surcharge for this service.

Bowl opened in 1916. The original shell was by Lloyd Wright, Frank's son, though the current design is by Frank Gehry.
✉ **2301 Highland Ave, Hollywood Hills ☎ 323-850 2000 [e] www.hollywoodbowl.org 🚌 MTA 420 ♿ OK**

Music Center of LA County
See page 85.

Orange County Performing Arts Center
The Music Center of LA County cringed at first, but is now comfortable sharing the area's classical music, ballet and opera scene with this venue.
✉ **behind South Coast Plaza, Costa Mesa (1, J7) ☎ 714-556 2787 🕒 box office 10am-6pm, and till ½hr after curtain $ student and rush tickets available**

CINEMAS
Aero
On a fun and fashionable shopping and dining street, $6 buys a double-bill at the historic Aero.
✉ **cnr Montana Ave & 14th St, Santa Monica (2, D1) ☎ 310-395 4990 🚌 SM 3**

Lowes Cineplex Fairfax Theaters
Shows new releases and charges just $2.75 for any ticket, any seat, any time.
✉ **cnr Beverly Blvd & Fairfax Blvd, W Hollywood (4, E3) ☎ 323-653 3117 🚌 MTA 4**

Nuart Theater
Revival and arthouse cinema famous for its Saturday midnight *Rocky Horror Picture Show* screenings.
✉ **cnr Santa Monica Blvd & Sawtelle St, W Hollywood (2, C1) ☎ 310-478 6379, 310-473 8530 after 5pm 🚌 MTA 4, 304; SM 5 $ first show Sat & Sun $5**

Westwood Theater
Also known as Mann Four Plex, the Westwood is among LA's most popular cinemas for studio previews. In a first-run moviehouse neighbourhood, it's a perfect destination if you want to browse what's playing.
✉ **1050 Gayley Ave, Westwood (2, C1) ☎ 310-208 7664 🚌 MTA 2, 302, 576; SM 3 $ $7/4.50**

Rick Gerharter

One of Westwood's many movie-houses

GAY & LESBIAN
7969
Outrageous erotic entertainment with a different theme every night; dress up and play the part.
✉ **7969 Santa Monica Blvd, W Hollywood (4, E2) ☎ 213-654 0280 🚌 MTA 4, 304 🕒 9.30pm-2am**

The Palms
Long-established lesbian bar with a consistent, low-key crowd.
✉ **8572 Santa Monica Blvd, W Hollywood (4, F1) ☎ 323-652 6188 🚌 MTA 4, 304 🕒 2pm-2am**

Rage
Trendy men's dance club where fashion slaves go to see and be seen. Look hip or forget about getting in.
✉ **8911 Santa Monica Blvd, W Hollywood (4, F2) ☎ 310-652 7055 🚌 MTA 4, 304 🕒 noon-2am**

SPORTS VENUES
Dodger Stadium
(3, A1) On the northern edge of Downtown, this baseball stadium is home to the LA Dodgers.
✉ **1000 Elysian Park Ave, Downtown ☎ 323-224 1400/1448 [e] www.dodgers.com 🚌 MTA 1, 2, 3, 4, 302, 304 🕒 box office Mon-Sat 8.30am-5.30pm $ $6-$13 (kids ½ price); parking $6**

Staples Center (3, J2)
Since autumn 1999, the LA Kings (NHL), LA Lakers (NBA) and LA Clippers (NBA) have shared one venue – the $300 million Staples Center, cornerstone of the revitalisation plan for Downtown.
✉ **1111 S Figueroa St, Downtown ☎ 310-673 1300 (stadium), 888-546 4752 (Kings), 310-419 3131 (Lakers), 213-745 0500 (Clippers) [e] www.staplescenterla.com 🚆 Blue Line to Pico or Grand 🚌 MTA 33, 65, 68, 333 🕒 box office 10am-6pm; centre open 1½hrs before games $ varies**

SAN FRANCISCO & BAY AREA

THEATRE & COMEDY

Beach Blanket Babylon at Club Fugazi

San Francisco's longest-running comedy extravaganza, known for its wild costumes and hilarious visual puns, is into its third decade and still packing them in.
✉ 678 Green St (Beach Blanket Babylon Blvd), North Beach (7, C2) ☎ 415-421 4222 🚌 Muni 30 🚋 Powell-Mason cable car 🕐 Wed-Thurs 8pm, Fri-Sat 7 & 10pm, Sun 3 & 7pm 👤 over 21s only, except Sun matinee

Greeting the punters at Beach Blanket Babylon, Club Fugazi

Cobb's Comedy Club

A team of 15 professional improvisational comics take to the stage Monday to Wednesday, a headliner performs Thursday to Saturday and Sunday is 'amateur' night. Ask about their dinner & show deals.
✉ The Cannery, 2801 Leavenworth St, Fisherman's Wharf (7, C1) ☎ 415-928 4320 🌐 www.ticketweb.com (ticketing service) 🚌 Muni 30, 32, 42 🚋 Powell-Hyde cable car 🕐 Mon-Wed 8pm, Thurs-Sun 8 & 10pm 👤 over 16s only (under 18s must be accompanied by an adult)

Finocchio's

The script hasn't changed much since this club's opening in 1936: female impersonators engage in a camp comedy routine that won't make even the faint-hearted blush. Still, it's an amusing, if docile, night's entertainment.
✉ 506 Broadway, North Beach (7, C3) ☎ 415-982 9388 (information), 415-362 9913 (after 7pm) 🚌 Muni 30 🚋 Powell-Mason cable car 🕐 Thurs-Sat 8.30, 10 & 11pm (doors open 7.45pm) 👤 over 21s only

Geary Theater

One of the first stages to open after the 1906 earthquake and fire, and extensively renovated after the 1989 earthquake, it remains central to the SF theatre scene. It is home to the acclaimed American Conservatory Theater (ACT) whose season extends September to April.
✉ 415 Geary St, Union Square (7, D4) ☎ 415-749 2228 🚋 BART Powell St 🚌 Muni 38 🕐 box office 10am-6pm $ rush tickets available for some performances

Orpheum, Golden Gate & Curran Theatres

This Union Square trio shares performances of contemporary music headliners, big spectacular shows – like the Andrew Lloyd-Webber musicals – and the Curran Theater's *Best of Broadway* series. The central box office is at the Orpheum.
✉ Orpheum: 1192 Market St (7, E4); Golden Gate: cnr Taylor & Golden Gate Sts (7, E4); Curran: 445 Geary St (7, D4) ☎ 415-551 2000 🌐 www.bestofbroadway-sf.com 🚋 BART Powell St 🚌 Muni 38 🕐 central box office Mon-Sat 10am-6pm, individual box offices 2hrs before show $ same-day and rush tickets from individual box offices, advanced sales through central box office

Punchline

Bill Graham's venture into the world of comedy created a club that still gets San Francisco's most contemporary and creative comedy acts. Dinner available.
✉ Maritime Plaza, Embarcadero Center (7, C4) ☎ 415-397 4337 (box office; 1-6pm), 415-397 7573 (recorded info), 415-397 0644 (parking & directions) 🚋 BART Embarcadero 🚌 Muni 1, 30, 42 🕐 Tues-Sun 9pm, Fri & Sat 11pm (doors open 8.30 & 10.45pm) 👤 over 18s only

BARS, PUBS & LOUNGES

Carnelian Room

At the top of the Bank of America Building, it provides the best views in the city. Patrons are well-heeled (many of them are members of the bank's private club).
✉ **52nd fl, Bank of America Bldg, 555 California St, Financial District (7, C4) ☎ 415-433 7500 🚋 C line cable car 🕘 Tues-Sat 5pm-1am**

Hayes & Vine

Beautiful, sophisticated but comfortable and unpretentious wine bar with a good selection of international wines.
✉ **377 Hayes St, Civic Center (7, F4) ☎ 415-626 5301 🚆 BART Civic Center 🚋 Muni to Van Ness 🕘 9pm-2am**

Perry's

Once the No 1 cruising spot for straight singles, it featured in Armistead Maupin's *Tales of the City* novels as the archetypal San Fran 'breeder' bar. The food is almost as big an attraction as the people-watching.
✉ **1944 Union St, Cow Hollow (7, E1) ☎ 415-922 9022 🚌 Muni 39 🕘 Mon-Tues 9am-10pm, Wed-Thurs 9am-11pm, Fri-Sat 9am-midnight**

Redwood Room

The Art Deco lounge of the classic Clift Hotel is popular for romantic rendezvous and business drinks. Just the place to sip martinis.
✉ **Clift Hotel, 496 Geary St at Taylor, Union Square (7, D4) ☎ 415-775 4700 🚆 BART Powell St 🚌 Muni 2, 3, 4 🕘 Sun-Thurs 11am-1am, Fri-Sat 11am-2am**

The Saloon

This worn-looking old bar was one of only 2 buildings in North Beach to survive the 1906 fire – the owners say it's been standing since 1861. Blues and 60s rock acts often perform here.
✉ **1232 Grant Ave, North Beach (7, C3) ☎ 415-989 7666 🚌 Muni 15, 30 🚋 Powell-Mason cable car 🕘 noon-2am**

Tosca Cafe

As famous for its people-watching opportunities as it is for the arias that emanate from the all-opera jukebox. Local literati are known to unwind here in the red vinyl diner booths.
✉ **242 Columbus Ave, North Beach (7, C3) ☎ 415-391 1244 🚌 Muni 15, 30 🚋 Powell-Mason cable car 🕘 5.30pm-1.30am**

Simon Bracken

Perry's famous bar

MUSIC & DANCE CLUBS

924 Gilman

The West Coast's most influential punk and alternative rock club. You needn't have a mohawk and mosh-pit desires to enjoy the raw, energetic sounds that come out of this graffiti-covered warehouse. All ages are allowed – but there's no alchohol.
✉ **924 Gilman St, Berkeley (5, B3) ☎ 510-525 9926, 510-524 8180 [e] www.gilman.org 🚌 AC Transit 9, 43, 52 🕘 shows start 8pm $ $5 cover charge**

Bimbo's 365 Club

One of the city's swankiest nightclubs, featuring everything from live swing and rockabilly to alternative rock, country and soul. Some big names also perform here.
✉ **cnr Columbus Ave & Chestnut St, North Beach (7, C2) ☎ 415-474 0365 🚌 Muni bus 30 🚋 Powell-Mason cable car 🕘 box office Mon-Fri 9am-4pm $ shows vary; 2-drink minimum**

Bottom of the Hill

Live music 7 nights a week; one of the hottest venues for up-and-coming bands. They also have a patio, pool table and all-you-can-eat BBQ on Sunday afternoon.
✉ **1233 17th St, The Mission (6, C4) ☎ 415-626 4455 🚌 Muni 22 🕘 Sun-Thurs 3pm-2am, Fri 2pm-2am, Sat 8pm-2am**

Cafe du Nord

Former 1930s speakeasy that combines jazz and

/est Coast blues at its
est. Tuesday is Latin music
ght, with free salsa danc-
g lessons at 9pm.
✉ **2170 Market St, The**
astro (7, H4) ☎ 415-
61 5016 🚇 Muni to
hurch St 🕘 6pm-2am,
/ed-Sun 4pm-2am;
usic from 9pm, food
ll 11pm

lub Deluxe
distinctly retro club
here the crowd dresses
e part, enjoying the
wing and big band tunes.
ne Tuesday night 'Rat
ack Cocktail Party' is a
ibute to Frank Sinatra and
magnet for young hip-
ers.
✉ **1511 Haight St,**
pper Haight (7, J2) ☎
15-552 6949 🚌 Muni
, 21, 50 🕘 Tues-Sun
pm-late

imball's East
n intimate supper club in
converted warehouse,
eaturing California cuisine,
nd top-name jazz, soul
nd R&B performers. The
over charge is waived if
ou have dinner before or
uring the show.
✉ **5800 Shellmound**
t, Emeryville (5, C3)
☎ 510-658 2555 🌐
/ww.kimballs.com 🚌
C Transit 6 or 57 to
meryville Amtrak sta-
on 🕘 box office Mon-
ri 12-6pm; doors open
.30pm, shows 8 &
0pm

loc Noc
ost-industrial, with a
pace-age, curving metal
ar and light fixtures, it
oks like the place where
ne crew from *Alien* would
ang out when they're on
arth.
✉ **557 Haight St,**
Lower Haight (7, G4)
☎ 415-861 5811 🚌
Muni 6, 7, 22, 66, 71
🕘 5pm-2am

Slim's
Authentic R&B club partly owned by 70s rock star Boz Scaggs; an impressive group of artists pass through – check the *Bay Guardian* for listings.
✉ **333 11th St, SoMa (7, F5) ☎ 415-621 3330 🚌 Muni 9, 42 🚇 Muni to Van Ness 🕘 8pm-2am $ $7-$24**

Sweetwater
A casual, intimate blues club that Bay Area residents adore. It's a low-key scene, but the music is outstanding and big-name performers have been known to drop in for a jam session.
✉ **138 Throckmorton Ave, Mill Valley (5, B2) ☎ 415-388 2820 🚌 Golden Gate Transit 10 to Mill Valley 🕘 5pm-late $ Mon free, Tues-Sun $5**

Up & Down Club
Hip spot to hear local jazz bands; Acid Jazz Thursday attracts a cool crew, and Saturday gets an inter-generational and ethnically diverse crowd for R&B, soul and hip-hop.
✉ **1151 Folsom St, SoMa (7, E5) ☎ 415-626 2388 🚌 Muni 12, 19 🕘 Thurs-Sun 9pm-1 or 2am; happy hour 9-10pm**

CLASSICAL MUSIC, DANCE & OPERA

Louise M Davies Symphony Hall
The rounded, glass-panel façade facing Van Ness is matched by the light-filled interior and excellent acoustics. The San Francisco Symphony performs September-May, other musical events are year-round.
✉ **cnr Van Ness Ave & Grove St, Civic Center (7, F4) ☎ 415-864 6000 🌐 www.sfsymphony.org 🚇 BART Civic Center 🚌 Muni 14, 26 🕘 box office Mon-Sat 10am-6pm $ student & senior rush tickets available (☎ 415-552 8011)**

War Memorial Opera House
Host to the acclaimed San Francisco Opera and San Francisco Ballet, it's in tip-top shape after a seismic refit. Following the 1989 earthquake, an enormous net was hung beneath the massive chandelier to

Holy Smoke!
Believe it or not, it is illegal to smoke in a bar in California. The smoking ban, which came into effect on New Year's Eve 1998, has been highly controversial and surprisingly successful. Most bars are enforcing the law, and state officials have fined some offenders. Meanwhile, smokers are finding it's not so difficult to step outside for a ciggie, bar employees are glad not to be breathing smoke all night and patrons are discovering hangovers are less severe when not compounded by second-hand smoke.

protect prime opera ticket holders.
✉ cnr Van Ness Ave & Grove St (7, F4) ☎ 415-864 3330 🅔 www.sfopera.com 🚇 BART Civic Center 🚊 Muni 14, 26 🕐 box office Mon-Fri 10am-6pm Ⓢ rush tickets available 2hrs before performances

Yerba Buena Center for the Arts
Ballet, contemporary dance companies (such as Lyons and Martha Graham), edgy issues-based theatre and classical music groups show their stuff.
✉ cnr Howard & 3rd Sts, Yerba Buena Gardens, SoMa (7, D5) ☎ 415-978 2787 🅔 www.yerbabuenaarts .org 🚇 BART Montgomery St 🚊 Muni 15, 30, 45; Golden Gate Transit 10, 20, 50, 60, 70, 80 to Folsom & 3rd Sts 🕐 box office Tues-Sat 11am-6pm

Zellerbach Hall
This wonderful space on the UC Berkeley campus presents rock acts but is also home to the Berkeley Symphony, and co-home to the San Francisco Ballet.
✉ south side, UC Berkeley campus, off Bancroft Ave (5, B3) ☎ 510-642 9988 🅔 www.calperf.berkeley.e du 🚇 BART Berkeley, then AC Transit bus 52 🕐 box office Mon-Fri 10am-5.30pm, Sat-Sun 10am-2pm Ⓢ rush tickets sometimes available

CINEMAS
Casting Couch
A self-proclaimed 'micro cinema', seating just 46

Sunday morning concert at Yerba Buena Gardens

people in its luxury loveseat couches. There's no need to queue for a choc-top; gourmet snacks are delivered to you.
✉ 950 Battery St, Fisherman's Wharf (7, B3) ☎ 415-986 7001 🅔 www.thecastingcouch.co m 🚊 Muni 42; Golden Gate Transit 30 Ⓢ $8.50

Castro Theater
Topping the list for cinemas where the building is as interesting as the film. A magnificent Wurlitzer organ rises out of the stage and the theatre has as much plush velvet, Grecian columns and fake plants as any vintage cinema buff can take.
✉ 429 Castro St, The

Castro (7, J4) ☎ 415-621 6120 🚊 Muni to Castro St Ⓢ $6.50/4; matinees $4

Clay Theatre
In business since 1913, it the longest continuously operating cinema in the city. It still looks magnificent, if a little careworn.
✉ cnr Fillmore & Clay Sts, Pacific Heights (7, F1) ☎ 415-346 1123 🚊 Muni 1 Ⓢ $7.50/4.75; matinee $4.75

Pacific Film Archive
The PFA's nightly screenings include international and classic films, ethnic and gender-specific festivals and rare foreign films
✉ 2575 Bancroft Way

Castro Theater, the historic icon of Castro St

erkeley (5, B3) ☎ 10-642 1124 🚆 BART erkeley, then AC trant bus No 8, 52, 65 🕘 dvanced sales Mon-Fri 1am-5pm from Durant ve box office; theatre ox office opens 1hr efore screenings $ 6/4

ed Vic
are cult films and other teresting oldies in a cooperively owned and managed ovie-house that continues be a favourite of urbanites.
✉ 1727 Haight St, pper Haight (7, J2) ☎ 15-668 3994 🚌 Muni , 21, 50 $ $6.50/3; pm shows $4.50

he Roxie
creens an adventurous, clectic selection of mainly assic, cult films, usually as series or theme-based equence.
✉ cnr 16th & Valencia ts, The Mission (7, G5) ☎ 415-863 1087 🚆 ART 16th & Mission 🚌 Muni 14, 22, 49 $ 7/3; 1st show Wed, at & Sun $4

JA Galaxy
he towering glass-and-teel complex is the city's rst, and one of its better, nultiplex cinemas. It's also ne of the few to show novies before noon.
✉ cnr Sutter St & Van Jess Ave, Nob Hill (7, 3) ☎ 415-474 8700, 15-474 8785 🚌 Muni ?, 3, 4, 42, 47, 49; Golden Gate Transit 10, 20, 60, 70, 80 $ 58/4.50; $5 before 6pm

JC Theatre
n the heart of downtown Berkeley and near a plethora of movie venues, this is one of the best of Berkeley's excellent arthouse cinemas with an eclectic menu of new, classic and camp films that changes nightly.
✉ 2036 University Ave, Berkeley (5, B3) ☎ 510-843 3456 🚆 BART Berkeley 🚌 AC Transit 52 $ $6.50/4.50

GAY & LESBIAN

The Cafe
One of the only places in The Castro with a dance floor, this place gets a young, ethnically diverse crowd that gets down and gets funky. An outdoor garden patio is good for cooling down and the large deck overlooking Market St is one of the city's prime people-watching spots.
✉ 2367 Market St, The Castro (7, J4) ☎ 415-861 3846 🚆 Muni Castro St 🕘 12.30pm-2am; dancing from 8pm; tea dancing Sun 3pm

CoCo Club
Not strictly a lesbian club, but a steady source of lesbian entertainment where dancing is only one facet of the constantly evolving scene. Call for current event information.
✉ cnr 8th & Minna Sts, SoMa (7, E5) ☎ 415-626 2337 🚆 BART Civic Center 🚌 Muni 12, 19

The Detour
A chain-link urban playground theme, superior sound system, go-go dancers and a diverse crowd make this a hot spot. It's also got great drink bargains, with $1 beers and shots on Sunday, and the longest happy hour around (2-8pm).
✉ 2348 Market St, The Castro (7, H4) ☎ 415-861 6053 🚆 Muni Castro St 🕘 2pm-2am

Endup
One of the most popular dance clubs in the city, particularly on its gay and lesbian nights (usually Friday and Saturday 9pm-2am, but call to check).
✉ cnr 6th & Harrison Sts, SoMa (7, E5) ☎ 415-357 0827 🚌 Muni 27, 42 🕘 10am-4am

Lexington Club
The city's only lesbian-only bar, a casual place with a juke box and cheap drinks.
✉ cnr 19th & Lexington Sts, The

Simon Bracken

The Cafe's balcony – the top spot to people-watch

Mission (6, E5) ☎ 415-863 2052 🚇 BART 16th & Mission 🚌 Muni 14, 19 ⏰ 3pm-2am

Twin Peaks Tavern

One of San Francisco's first gay bars; the owner pioneered large bay windows so the patrons could watch the passing scene. ✉ cnr Castro & Market Sts, The Castro (7, J4) ☎ 415-864 9470 🚌 Muni Castro St ⏰ noon-2am

SPORTS VENUES

3Com Park (formerly Candlestick Park)

Built in 1960, 'the Stick' is known for being cold, foggy and windy. Home to the 49ers (NFL) and Giants (MLB), the stadium takes its food seriously – try a Polish sausage or 12-clove garlic chicken sandwich washed down with a Gordon Biersch brew. ✉ Jamestown Ave, Candlestick Point (off map) ☎ 415-656 4949 (stadium), 415-468 2249 (49ers), 415-468 3700 (Giants) 🌐 www.3com.com/3compark/ 🚇 BART to Colma, then SamTrans bus No 82F 🚌 Muni Ballpark Express 9x, 28x, 49x (direct service) ⏰ box office Mon-Fri 9am-5pm

Oakland Coliseum

Designed by the renowne architecture firm Skidmore Owings & Merrill, this sports complex was built 1966. The Athletics baseball team, Golden State Warriors (NBA) and Raide (NFL) call it home. ✉ 7000 Coliseum Way, Oakland (5, C3) ☎ 510-569 2121 (stadium & Warriors info), 510-638 4900 (Athletics), 800-949 2626 (Raiders) 🌐 www.oaklandathletics .com; www.raiders .org 🚇 BART to Oakland Coliseum ⏰ box office Mon-Fri 10am-6pm, Sat 10am-4pm

Spectator Sports

California has more professional teams than any other US state and a climate that allows most events to be held outside.

American Football California has 3 National Football League (NFL) teams: the San Diego Chargers; the San Francisco 49ers; and the Oakland Raiders. The teams have good records, though the 49ers are generally superior and have won 5 Superbowls.

The season runs from mid-August to Superbowl Sunday (2nd weekend in January); each team plays 1 game a week. It's almost impossible to get tickets to 49ers games; Raiders and Chargers tickets are easier to come by.

Baseball California's 5 Major League Baseball (MLB) teams are: the LA Dodgers; California (Anaheim) Angels; San Diego Padres; San Francisco Giants; and Oakland A's. Each team plays 162 games (as many as 5 per week) from April to October.

With so many games, tickets are cheap and relatively easy to secure. The Web site at www.majorleaguebaseball.com is a good source of information.

Basketball California has 4 NBA teams: the Sacramento Kings; LA Lakers; LA Clippers; and Golden State (Oakland) Warriors. While the Warriors rarely do well, the Kings and Lakers have had many winning seasons. Teams play around 80 games during the September-April season; playoffs are in May and the world championship is in June.

Beach Volleyball Beach towns in LA host several professional beach volleyball tournaments each summer – the Hermosa Open and Manhattan Open are the most important. Entrance is free and a beach party scene pervades. You'll find professionals practicing and playing daily at 16th St, Hermosa Beach, and Marine St, Manhattan Beach.

;AN DIEGO

'HEATRE & :OMEDY

'he Comedy Store

mall and mellow, this La ɔlla club has a good cast f regulars and gets come- ians from around outhern California.
✉ 916 Pearl St, La olla (8, C1) ☎ 858- ·54 9176 🚌 MTS 34, ·4A, 34B 🕘 Mon-Sat ·pm, Sun 8.30pm $ Aon-Thurs free, Fri-Sun ·10 (all nights 2-drink ninimum) 👶 OK

.a Jolla Playhouse ıt UCSD

stablished in 1947 by La olla native Cary Grant, its ummer season has pro- luced such Broadway hits s *Tommy* and *A Walk ɿ the Woods.*
✉ Mandell Weiss :enter for the 'erforming Arts, UCSD :ampus, La Jolla (8, B2) ☎ 858-550 1070 [e] vww.lajollaplayhouse com 🚌 MTA 34, 34A, ·4B 🕘 noon-8pm on ɔerformance days $ ·tudent & senior rush ometimes available

·imon Edison Center 'or the Performing \rts (9, A5)

'hree theatres in Balboa 'ark including The Old ilobe, which has a popular ummer Shakespeare series nd a world-class costume lepartment.
✉ El Prado, Balboa Park ☎ 619-239 2255 [e] vww.oldglobe.org 🚌 ATS 5, 15, 20, 20A, 20B, '10, 270, 810, 820, 850, ·60 🕘 box office Tues- ·un 12-8.30pm $ stu- lent and senior rush tick- ·ts sometimes available

BARS, PUBS & LOUNGES

The Bitter End

Once a brothel, now an upscale but easy-going bar that prides itself on out- standing bartenders and excellent martinis. The 3- 7pm happy hour draws a big, yuppy crowd. Smart attire required.
✉ 770 5th Ave at F St, Gaslamp Quarter (9, E4) ☎ 619-338 9300 🚌 MTS 1, 3, 4, 5, 16, 25 🕘 3pm-2am

Moondoggie's

A large outside patio, multi- ple big screen TVs, pool tables and large tap selec- tion make this a popular hangout. The food – burgers, salads, pastas and fried things – is very good, and Thursday to Saturday you'll often find live bands playing.
✉ 832 Garnet Ave, Pacific Beach (8, E2) ☎ 858-483 6550 🚌 MTS 27, 30, 34, 34A, 34B 🕘 11am-1am (Fri-Sat till 2am)

The Waterfront

Keeper of San Diego's first liquor licence, it was actu- ally on the waterfront until San Diego's harbour was filled in and the airport built. There's a big window that opens onto the street, $5 bar food and live music on weekends.
✉ 2044 Kettner Blvd, Little Italy (9, B2) ☎ 619-232 9656 🚌 MTS 5, 16 🚆 Blue Line to County Center/Little Italy 🕘 6am-2am

LIVE MUSIC

The Belly Up Tavern

A converted hangar decked with colourful, oversized paintings, it is one of the city's most intimate and lively music venues. Nightly themes include dance-house reggae and disco; travelling bands appear several nights a week.
✉ 143 South Cedros Ave, Solana Beach (1, K7) ☎ 858-481 9022 🚆 Amtrak/Coaster to Solana Beach 🚌 MTS 308, 310 🕘 doors open 6pm; food Mon-Sat 11.30am-2.30pm & 6-11pm, Sun 9am-9pm

Cafe Sevilla

Tapas bar with live flamen- co and rhumba guitarists nightly, Friday and Saturday flamenco dinner shows (7.30pm) and late-night dancing to contemporary funk-house-techno-disco- pop in the underground Club Sevilla; tapas is served until 1am.
✉ 555 4th Ave, Gaslamp Quarter (9, E4) ☎ 619-233 5979 🚌 MTS 1, 3, 5, 16, 25 🕘 happy hour 5-7pm; music from 9pm

Croce's Top Hat Bar & Grill

Run by the family of the late bluesman Jim Croce, this is San Diego's best R&B venue. The adjacent restaurant and jazz bar gets additional performers and serves good seafood, BBQ and American cuisine.
✉ 802 5th Ave, Gaslamp Quarter (9, E4) ☎ 619-233 4355 🚌 MTS 1, 3, 4, 5, 16, 25 🕘 R&B 8.30pm-12.30am, jazz bar 9.30-11.30pm $ $5 cover most nights

Milligan's
The well-kept piano bar of this high-end restaurant has mellow music on Sunday, Tuesday and Wednesday. It comes alive Thursday-Saturday with the sounds of jazz legend Bobby Gordon and his buddies.
✉ 5786 La Jolla Blvd, La Jolla (8, D1) ☎ 858-459 7311 🚌 MTS 34, 34A 🕒 music 7-11pm

CLASSICAL MUSIC, DANCE & OPERA

Mandeville Auditorium
Home of the highly acclaimed La Jolla Symphony (Nov-May), the San Diego Chamber Chorus and guest performances.
✉ La Jolla Village Dr, UCSD Campus (8, B2) ☎ 858-534 4637 🚌 MTS 34, 34A, 34B 🕒 Mon-Fri 9am-5pm $ rush tickets sold 1hr before curtain

San Diego Civic Theater (9, D3)
Performances by the California Ballet and the San Diego Opera which, under the wand of small but powerful Karen Keltner, has hosted such stars as Placido Domingo, José Carreras and Cecilia Bartoli.
✉ 202 3rd Ave at B St, Downtown ☎ 619-570 1100 (opera), 619-560 6741 (ballet) [e] www.sdcivic.com 🚌 MTS 1, 3, 5, 11, 16, 25 🚊 Civic Center 🕒 box office Mon-Fri 9am-5pm (by phone 10am-3pm) $ rush tickets sold 1½hrs before curtain

CINEMAS

Hillcrest Cinemas
In the postmodern Village Hillcrest Center, surrounded by shops and restaurants, the 5 theatres show some European and classic movies, as well as current releases.
✉ 3965 5th Ave, Hillcrest (8, F4) ☎ 619-299 2100 🚌 MTS 1, 8, 11, 16 along University Ave $ $7.75/5

Pacific Gaslamp 15
Along with the 7-theatre United Artists complex in Horton Plaza, this slick new compound is the main downtown movie venue, with 15 theatres showing current releases.
✉ cnr 5th Ave & G St, Gaslamp Quarter (9, E4) ☎ 619-232 0400 🚌 MTS to Gaslamp Quarter $ $8/5-5.50; early shows $5

GAY & LESBIAN

Club Bombay
Lesbian club with DJs and dancing on Friday night and live bands on Saturday night. It's a mellow but fun scene.
✉ 3175 India St, Little Italy (9, A2) ☎ 619-296 6789 🚌 MTS 5, 16 🚊 Blue Line to County Center/Little Italy 🕒 4pm-2am

Kickers
A popular gay dance club. Tuesday is 80s night, Wednesday-Saturday is mostly country & western and Sunday is a hip-hop extravaganza.
✉ 308 University Ave, Hillcrest (8, F4) ☎ 619-491 0400 🚌 MTS 1, 8, 11, 16 🕒 7pm-2am

SPORTS VENUES

Qualcomm Stadium (8, E5) Home to the San Diego Padres baseball team and San Diego Chargers football team, it is well-serviced by public transport.
✉ 9449 Friars Road, Mission Valley ☎ 619-641 3131 (stadium), 619-283 7294 (Padres), 619-280 2111 (Chargers) [e] www.padres.org; www.chargers.com 🚊 Blue Line to Qualcomm Stadium 🕒 box office Mon-Fri 9am-6pm, Sat 10am-4pm (till 10pm game days)

San Diego Sports Arena (8, F3)
Besides being home to the San Diego Gulls (hockey) and San Diego Stingrays (basketball), the arena is San Diego's largest indoor

Cinema Under the Stars

Modelled after Italian outdoor cinemas, San Diego's **Garden Cabaret** is an extremely enjoyable place to see a movie. The program is usually heavy on Hollywood classics and films with contemporary significance.

The season runs from June to August. Shows start at 8.30pm and cost $8; you can reserve a table ($2) at which to consume the coffee, tea, designer sodas, decadent desserts and popcorn on offer. Call the box office (☎ 619-295 4221) or stop by the theatre, 4040 Goldfinch St, Hillcrest (8, F4), for show information.

concert venue.
✉ 3350 Sports Arena Blvd (8, F3) ☎ 619-224 4171 (box office), 619-224 4176 (events hotline) [e] www.sandiegoarena.com 🚌 MTS 26, 34 🕘 box office Mon-Fri 10am-5pm, Sat 10am-3pm; doors open 1hr before events

Daily theatrics, Columbia State Historic Park

Stages of Gold

Several Gold Country towns have surprisingly good, prolific live theatre groups. In **Nevada City** the professional Foothill Theatre Company (☎ 530-265 9320) and Cheap Suit Productions (☎ 530-478 0929) both use the Miners Foundry Cultural Center and Nevada Theater as venues. The Off Broadstreet Theater (☎ 530-265 8686), 305 Commercial St, is a 'dessert theatre' which presents mostly adult comedies.

Sonora's Stage 3 Theater (☎ 209-536 1778) does off-Broadway and contemporary dramas, while the Foundry Playhouse (☎ 209-532 0345) has musicals, dramas and some locally-written stuff in the old foundry.

At **Columbia State Historic Park**, the Sierra Repertory Theater (☎ 209-532 3120) stages contemporary productions – usually musicals – in the old Fallon Hotel. Shows run year-round, Wednesday to Sunday.

AROUND CALIFORNIA

EUREKA (1, B2)

Ritz Club

A long-time Eureka institution, known for its stiff cocktails, unsophisticated local scene and DJ dance music Thursday to Saturday nights.
✉ cnr 3rd & F Sts ☎ 707-445 8577 🚌 Eureka Transit to Old Town Eureka 🕘 Mon-Fri 11am-2am, Sat 2pm-2am, Sun 5pm-2am

GOLD COUNTRY (1, D4)

Magic Theater

Perhaps the smallest, friendliest and most sustainable movie-house in California. The 'escaped from LA' owner serves popcorn in real bowls, coffee in real mugs and bakes brownies for intermission (required because the projector can only handle one reel of film at a time).
✉ 107 Argall Way, Nevada City ☎ 530-265 8262 🕘 8pm $ Mon-Thurs $3, Fri-Sun $4

LAKE TAHOE (1, D5)

Elevation

North Lake Tahoe's most lively venue for funk, reggae and swing. DJs play when there's no live show – check *North Tahoe Truckee Week* and the Action section of *Tahoe World* for listings.
✉ N Lake Tahoe Blvd, Tahoe City ☎ 530-583 4867 🚌 TART to Boatworks Mall 🕘 doors open 6pm, shows start 9/10pm

PALM SPRINGS (1, J8)

Plaza Theater

Home of the famous Palm Springs Follies revue, which includes music, showgirls and comedy. The twist is that all the performers are over 50, but this is far from amateur hour.
✉ 128 S Palm Canyon Dr ☎ 760-327 0225, 760-864 3252 🕘 Nov-May 8.30pm $ $27-$65

The Tool Shed

A hot and sweaty gay dance scene, though patrons claim that the people-watching and blended cocktails are just as important. Dress to impress.
✉ 600 E Sunny Dunes Rd ☎ 760-320 3299 🕘 Mon-Thurs 8am-2am, Fri-Sat 8am-4am, Sun 6am-2am

SAN LUIS OBISPO (1, G5)

Performance Arts Center

Pride of San Luis Obispo, the new $30 million, ultra-cool building by Albert Bertoli is styled after a European opera house and offers fine acoustics for music and dance.
✉ California Polytechnic State University Campus ☎ 805-756 2787 [e] www.pacslo.org 🚌 SLO Transit from downtown 🕘 box

office Mon-Fri 10am-6pm, Sat 10am-4pm

SANTA BARBARA (1, H5)

Arlington Theater

Home to the Arlington Center for the Performing Arts and the Santa Barbara Symphony, the theatre shows ballet, light opera and orchestral music.
✉ 1317 State St ☎ 805-963 4408 🚌 22 🕘 box office Mon-Fri 9am-6pm $ student rush available

Lobero Theater

California's oldest continuously operating theatre is home to the Lobero Theater Foundation and Santa Barbara Chamber Orchestra, and presents musicals, comedies, children's theatre and films.
✉ 33 E Cañon Perdido St ☎ 805-963 0761 🚌 22 🕘 box office Mon-Sat 10am-6pm $ senior discounts & student rush available for most performances

The Palm

Old-style movie-house in the heart of Santa Barbara that shows foreign and classic films nightly.
✉ 817 Palm St ☎ 805-541 5161 $ $6; Mon $3

Soho

Live jazz nightly in a friendly, intimate atmosphere. The usual cover charge is waived on Monday nights. No beach clothes allowed.
✉ 1221 State St ☎ 805-962 7776 🚋 Trolley to Paseo Nuevo 🕘 Sun-Thurs 5-11.30pm, Fri-Sat 5pm-2am

SANTA CRUZ (1, F3)

Blue Lagoon

Popular with the local gay crowd, students and anyone seeking loud techno and retro tunes.
✉ 923 Pacific Ave ☎ 831-423 7117 🕘 Mon-Sat 4pm-1.45am, Sun 2pm-1.45am

Palookaville

A well-known bar/dance venue among other nightspots on Santa Cruz's Pacific Ave. The cover charge is often high but the musos playing here are superior to most around town. All ages welcome.
✉ 1133 Pacific Ave ☎ 831-454 0600 🚌 SCMTD 1 to 12 🕘 doors open 8.30pm, music starts 9pm $ $18-$26

WINE COUNTRY

Rainbow Cattle Company

Probably the best gay bar in the Russian River nightlife scene; the summer sizzles, the winter is decidedly more dull.
✉ 16220 Main St, Guerneville (1, D2) ☎ 707-869-0206 🕘 6am-2am

Tamale Malone's Cantina

Mexican food, wicked margaritas and something going on every night; it's especially lively on weekends. Drink specials and free appetisers are part of happy hour (4-6pm).
✉ 245 Healdsburg Ave, Healdsburg (1, D3) ☎ 707-431 1856 🕘 11.30am-late

Laguna Arts Festival

The much-celebrated Festival of Arts held in Laguna Beach, Orange County, presents high quality arts and crafts and fine art auctions in July and August. The best-loved attraction is the nightly Pageant of the Masters, where actors portray well-known artworks.

Tickets for the pageant are $10-$50 and can sell out far in advance, especially for Friday, Saturday and Sunday nights. All shows are at 8.30pm. Other arts festival venues are open daily 10am-11.30pm and cost $5 (free with a Pageant of the Masters ticket). Call ☎ 949-497 6582 or 800-487 3378 for tickets, or check out the festival Web site (www.foapom.com).

Seeing is believing: a live actor gets into her art at the Pageant of the Masters

places to stay

There's a huge array of accommodation in California, with good options in every price range. While each region has places that reflect the local character – postmodern boutique hotels in LA, refurbished Victorian B&Bs in San Francisco, rustic inns in Big Sur, beach cottages in San Diego – these are the exceptions to the norm. The standard room you'll find from La Jolla to Arcata will have a TV, telephone, private bathroom (with soap and shampoo), climate control, and clean sheets and towels. Other amenities might include a swimming pool, coin laundry, continental breakfast and free local calls.

Room rates depend mostly on the bed configuration, not on how many people occupy the room. Rooms with a view naturally cost extra. Seasonal price fluctuations are common, with rates leaping up from late May to mid-September in most places (except ski resorts and the desert) – sometimes by more than 50%. On weekends, year-round, hotels catering to business travellers often have special deals. Discounts of 10% or more are frequently available if you are a member of the AAA or one of its foreign affiliates, a senior citizen, in the military or on business. Many motels advertise that 'kids stay free', but you will have to pay extra for a baby cot or a 'rollaway' (portable bed). Most places require a credit-card number to book a room; let them know if you plan on a late arrival (after 5pm).

Tom Downs

Room Rates

The price ranges in this chapter indicate the cost per night of a standard double with two-person occupancy in the high season.

$	$99
$$	$100-$179
$$$	$180-$240
$$$$	over $240

airmont Hotel – old-school values atop San Francisco's Nob Hill (p. 101)

B&B-ware

North American B&Bs differ markedly from the casual, inexpensive sorts of places found in Europe. While they are usually family-run, many, if not most, require advance bookings, prohibit smoking and are frequented by the well-heeled. Sometimes proprietors charge per person rather than per room, so be sure you know the correct rate before getting settled.

For a list of California's B&Bs, contact **B&B International**, (☎ 408-867 9662, 800-872 4500; fax 408-867 0907; www.bbinto.com), 12711 McCartisville Place, Saratoga CA 95070. This organisation also makes reservations at any of its 400 member B&Bs for $10 per booking.

LOS ANGELES

Beverly Hills Hotel $$$$

Splendour has been restored to this legendary hotel, thanks to a $100 million face-lift in the early 1990s – courtesy of the current owner, the Sultan of Brunei.

✉ 9641 Sunset Blvd, Beverly Hills (4, J1) ☎ 310-276 2251; fax 887 2887 🚌 MTA 2 ✕ Polo Lounge

Cadillac Hotel $

One of the best bargains in LA, this Art Deco landmark is right in Venice's heart. Rooms have ocean views, and there's a gym, sauna and rooftop sundeck.

✉ 8 Dudley Ave, Venice (2, E1) ☎ 310-399 8876; fax 399 4536 🚌 MTA 4, 20, 22, 33

Carlyle Inn $$

Service here is superb, and rates include breakfast buffet, afternoon tea, cocktails and a free shuttle service within a 5-mile radius.

✉ 1119 S Robertson Blvd, Beverly Hills (4, G4) ☎ 310-275 4445; fax 859 0496 🌐 www.carlyle-inn.com 🚌 MTA 10

Casa Malibu Inn $$

A lovely spot overlooking a private beach. Some of the 21 rooms have decks, fireplaces and kitchenettes.

✉ 22752 Pacific Coast Hwy, Malibu (1, J6) ☎ 310-456 2219; fax 456 5418 🌐 www.malibu.com

Château Marmont $$$

The Marmont is a favourite celebrity hideaway, thanks to its Norman castle design, gorgeous gardens, special services (including complimentary mobile phones) and legendary discretion.

✉ 8221 Sunset Blvd, Hollywood (4, G1) ☎ 323-656 1010; fax 655 5311 🚌 MTA 2, 3 to Crescent Heights ✕ Bar Marmont

Hotel Figueroa $-$$

A 1927 Spanish-style classic, whose lobby evokes an oversized hacienda. Spacious rooms have all amenities and a reasonable price tag. It's very popular, so call ahead.

✉ 939 S Figueroa St, Downtown (3, J2) ☎ 213-627 8971; fax 689 0305 🚌 DASH C ✕ Pasta Firenze, The Music Room

Spanish charm of the Hotel Figueroa

David Peevers

Hotel Queen Mary $$-$$$

Experience the atmosphere of a classic ocean liner in the original (refurbished), but somewhat cramped, staterooms of this permanently moored vessel. The portholes don't provide too much light, but the mood of Art Deco afloat is unrivalled.

✉ 1126 Queens Hwy, Long Beach Harbor (2, H5) ☎ 562-435 3511; fax 437 4531 🌐 www.queenmary.com 🚉 Blue Line to Long Beach then free Passport Shuttle ✕ 3 onboard restaurants

Hotel Shangri-La $$

Housed in a swanky 1939 Art Deco building, this hotel has long been a sentimental favourite with celebs. Rooms are outfitted with retro-style furniture, and some with kitchenettes. Rates include continental breakfast and afternoon tea.

✉ 1301 Ocean Ave, Santa Monica (2, D1) ☎ 310-394 2791; fax 310-451 3351 🌐 www.shangrila-hotel.com 🚌 MTA 22, 33

Le Montrose $$$$

A cosy hideaway with a $2 million art collection and 120 large suites, each with sunken living room and fireplace. Views from the rooftop swimming pool, framed by private cabanas, are breathtaking.

✉ 900 Hammond St, W Hollywood (4, G1) ☎ 310-855 1115; fax 657 9192 🌐 www.lemontrose.com 🚌 MTA 2 ✕ The Library

Mondrian $$$$

Like the gates to heaven, 2 giant doors admit you to LA's ultimate place for celeb sightings. It oozes exclusivity and sophistication, served

with a gallon of attitude –
it's just sooooo LA.

📧 8440 Sunset Blvd, W
Hollywood (4, F1) ☎
323-650 8999; fax 650
5215 🅴 www.mondri
anhotel.com 🚌 MTA 2
🍴 Asia to Cuba, Sky Bar

Ocean Lofts at
the Beach $$$
Just steps from the sand,
the gray-shingled lofts offer
separate living and bed-
room areas with balconies
overlooking the action-
packed Strand.

📧 1300 The Strand,
Hermosa Beach (2, G2)
☎ 310-374 3001; fax
372 2115 🅴 www.bea
ch-house.com 🚌 MTA
439

Regent Beverly
Wilshire $$$$
For a bit of old world flair,
check into the hotel from
which Julia Roberts first
stumbled, then sashayed,
in *Pretty Woman*. Luxury
is taken very seriously here;
many of the 285 rooms
have 2 bathrooms.

📧 9500 Wilshire Blvd,
Beverly Hills (4, H3) ☎
310-275 5200; fax 274
2851 🅴 www.foursea
sons.com 🚌 MTA 20 🍴
Lobby Lounge & Bar,
The Regent

Shutters on the
Beach $$$$
The only Santa Monica
hotel to be practically built
into the sand, the rooms

have fireplaces, private spa
and books, magazines and
videos.

📧 1 Pico Blvd, Santa
Monica (2, D1) ☎ 310-
458 0030; fax 458 4589
🅴 www.shuttersonthe
beach.com 🚌 MTA 22,
33 🍴 Shutters

The Standard   S-$$$
An ultra-sleek, minimalist,
modernist hotel. Wear
black, trade in your Ray
Bans for something more
Euro and come for a
martini at the no-name bar,
even if you don't stay.

📧 8300 Sunset Blvd,
Hollywood (4, E1) ☎
323-650 9090; fax 650
2820 🚌 MTA 2 🍴 The
Restaurant

SAN FRANCISCO & BAY AREA

Bancroft Hotel   S-$$
Directly opposite the UC
Berkeley campus and adja-
cent to the terrific Caffe
Strada, the Bancroft has 22
comfortable rooms.

📧 2680 Bancroft Way,
Berkeley ☎ 510-549
1000; fax 549 1070
🅴 reservation@bancr
ofthotel.com; www.ba
ncrofthotel.com 🚌 AC
Transit 52

Claremont Resort &
Spa $$$$
Indulge in a spa without
leaving the Bay Area.
Rooms are in an historic
1918 building, and there's
massage, a gym and swim-
ming pools at guests' dis-
posal. Various spa package
deals are available.

📧 cnr Ashby & Domin-
go Aves, Berkeley ☎
510-843 7924; fax 549

8582 🅴 reservation@clr
mntresort.com; www.cl
aremontresort.com
🚌 AC Transit 7 🍴 5
on-site eateries

Clift Hotel $$$
The Clift has been known
for stand-out service since
it opened in 1915; the
rooms have been mod-
ernised and refurbished,
but the attention to detail
hasn't diminished.

📧 495 Geary St, Union
Square (7, D4) ☎ 415-
775 4700; fax 931 7417
🅴 www.clifthotel.com
🚇 BART Powell St 🚈
Muni 2, 3, 4 🍴 The
Redwood Room (p. 90)

Fairmont
Hotel $$$-$$$$
A perfect remnant of the
days of steamer-trunk travel,
the Fairmont is seductively
smooth and resolutely old-
school. The cocktail lounges
are reason enough to stay –

he Chain Gang
he majority of California's motels are affiliated with
vell-publicised national chains, and most of them
uddle together around freeway exits. The reserva-
on numbers of some of the best known chains are:

Motel 6	☎ 800-466 8356
ʾays Inn	☎ 800-329 7466
ravelodge	☎ 800-578 7878
hoice Hotels	☎ 800-424 4777
uper 8 Motel	☎ 800-800 8000
est Western	☎ 800-528 1234
loward Johnson	☎ 800-446 4656

or at least pay a visit.
✉ **950 Mason St, Nob Hill (7, D3)** ☎ 415-772 5000; fax 772 5086 ⊜ www.fairmont.com 🚋 Powell-Hyde cable car ✗ 4 restaurants

Hotel Bohème $$
Small, stylish, with subdued decor that makes subtle reference to the area's Beat history. All rooms have a private bath.
✉ **444 Columbus Ave, North Beach (7, C3)** ☎ 415-433 9111; fax 362 6292 ⊜ www.hotelboheme.com 🚌 Muni 30

Hyatt Regency San Francisco $$$-$$$$
San Francisco's most architecturally memorable hotel, with a backward-leaning 20-storey atrium and revolving restaurant/bar. Its 800 rooms cater mostly to business travellers.
✉ **5 Embarcadero Center (7, C4)** ☎ 415-788 1234; fax 398 2567 ⊜ www.hyatt.com/pages/s/sforsba.html 🚇 BART Embarcadero 🚌 Muni Embarcadero ✗ 1 cafe, 2 restaurants

Inn at Union Square $$-$$$
All 30 elegantly old-fashioned rooms and suites are non-smoking. Rates include a continental breakfast, afternoon tea and wine.
✉ **440 Post St, Union Square (7, D4)** ☎ 415-397 3510; fax 989 0529 ⊜ www.unionsquare.com 🚇 BART Powell St 🚌 Muni 2, 3, 4

Inn San Francisco $-$$$
Housed in an 1872 mansion, this grand Victorian B&B has deluxe rooms

with fireplaces, spas or hot tubs; all guests have access to the gardens and rooftop deck.
✉ **943 S Van Ness Ave, The Mission (6, D5)** ☎ 415-641 0188; fax 641 1701 ⊜ www.innsf.com 🚇 BART 24th & Mission

Mandarin Oriental San Francisco $$$$
With its 158 rooms on the 38th to 48th floors of the city's third-highest building, this hotel offers spectacular views – even from the bathtubs – and many high-end amenities.
✉ **222 Sansome St, Financial District (7, C4)** ☎ 415-885 0999; fax 433 0289 ⊜ www.mandarin-oriental.com/hotels/MOSanFrancisco/location.html 🚇 BART Montgomery St 🚌 Muni 12, 15 ✗ Silks, Mandarin Lounge

Mark Hopkins Inter-Continental Hotel $$$-$$$$
Even among its high-end brethren atop Nob Hill, 'the Mark' is the quintessential San Francisco society place to stay. The building is a city landmark, and the cocktail lounge is renowned for its

superb bay views.
✉ **999 California St, Nob Hill (7, D3)** ☎ 415-392 3434; fax 421 3302 ⊜ hotels.san-francisco.interconti.com 🚇 BART Powell St 🚌 Muni 1 🚋 Powell-Hyde & C Line cable cars

Petite Auberge $$-$$$
With character poised somewhere between hotel and B&B, this intimate place is garnished with romantic details, and provides continental breakfast.
✉ **863 Bush St, Union Square (7, D3)** ☎ 415-928 6000; fax 775 5717 ⊜ www.vacations.com/four-sisters-inns/petite-auberge.htm 🚇 BART Powell St 🚌 Muni 2, 3, 4 ✗ La Petite Auberge

Stanyan Park Hotel $-$$
The sole remaining hotel from Golden Gate Park's glory days, the Stanyan is a fine Victorian building with quiet rooms and suites.
✉ **750 Stanyan St, Golden Gate Park (7, J2)** ☎ 415-751 1000; fax 668 5454 ⊜ www.stanyanpark.com 🚌 Muni 6, 7, 33 🚋 Muni N

Sumptuous lobby of the Triton Hotel, San Francisco

Triton Hotel $$
The Triton kick-started San Francisco's designer-hotel trend, and is notable for its 140 exotically designed guestrooms – including the Carlos Santana and Jerry Garcia suites.
✉ 342 Grant Ave, Chinatown (7, D4) ☎ 415-394 0500; fax 394 0555 🌐 www.hotel-tritonsf.com 🚇 BART Montgomery St 🚃 C Line & Powell St cable cars ✗ Cafe de la Presse

Tuscan Inn $$
This 220-room luxury hotel is much larger than it looks and feels, making it one of the nicest places to stay on the wharf.
✉ 425 North Point St, Fisherman's Wharf (7, C1) ☎ 415-561 1100; fax 292 4549 🌐 www.tuscaninn.com 🚇 Muni 30, 42 ✗ Cafe Pescatore

Westin St Francis Hotel $$$-$$$$
One of the city's most famous hotels, the St Francis occupies the entire west side of Union Square – the grand lobby, tea room and boutiques at ground level, and rooms towering above.
✉ 335 Powell St, Union Square (7, D4) ☎ 415-397 7000; fax 774 0124 🌐 www.westin.com 🚃 Powell St cable cars ✗ Dewey's, St Francis Cafe

SAN DIEGO

The Bed & Breakfast Inn at La Jolla $$
A San Diego classic, this 1913 Irving Gill house with Kate Sessions garden boasts 16 rooms with all the finest trimmings. The location is unbeatable – walking distance to most La Jolla sights.
✉ 7753 Draper Ave, La Jolla (8, D1) ☎ 858-456 2066 🚇 MTS 34, 34A, 34B

Best Western Hacienda Hotel $$
Handy to the San Diego trolley and Old Town's shops and restaurants, this Spanish-style hotel has suites with basic kitchens, a pool, gym and spa.
✉ 4041 Harney St, Old Town (8, F3) ☎ 619-298 4707; fax 298 4771 🌐 www.haciendahotel-oldtown.com 🚇 MTS to Old Town 🚃 Blue Line to Old Town ✗ Acapulco

Catamaran Resort Hotel $$-$$$
One of the first and finest of the Mission Bay resorts, it has a terrific Polynesian-style bar, pool, boat, bike and skate rentals, and nightly cruises on the *Bahia Belle* sternwheeler.
✉ 3999 Mission Blvd, Mission Bay (8, E1) ☎ 858-488 1081; fax 488 1619 🌐 www.catamaran.com 🚇 MTS 27, 30, 34, 34A, 34B ✗ Atoll, Cannibal Bar

Crystal Pier Hotel $$
Whimsical cottages on Crystal Pier, perched right above the ocean. Dating from 1927, the distinctive arched entrance to the pier is a landmark at the end of Garnet Ave.
✉ 4500 Ocean Blvd, Pacific Beach (8, E1) ☎ 858-483 6983; fax 483 6811 🌐 www.crystalpier.com 🚇 MTS 27, 30, 34, 34A, 34B

Horton Grand Hotel $-$$
The Grand is more nostalgic than historic, but lots of people like the lace curtains and gas-fuelled fireplaces; ask about special rates before you book.
✉ 311 Island Ave,

Hotels run by national chains tend to be more centrally located, have more amenities and are more expensive. They include:

Radisson	☎ 800-333 3333
Hyatt	☎ 800-233 1234
Holiday Inn	☎ 800-465 4329
Marriott	☎ 800-228 9290
Sheraton	☎ 800-325 3535

The Hollywood Roosevelt Hotel (p. 35) is part of the Radisson chain.

Gaslamp Quarter (9, E4) ☎ 619-544 1886; fax 544 0058 ❸ www.hortongrand.com 🚍 MTS 1, 4, 11, 29, 901, 902, 903 🚊 Orange Line ✕ Ida Bailey's

Hotel del Coronado $$-$$$$

Edward, Prince of Wales, and Wallis Simpson started their affair here, 13 US Presidents have slept here and *Some Like it Hot* was partly filmed here. But, ignoring the hype, nearly half the rooms are in an adjacent modern building with no historical feel at all, and the rooms in the original timber building are pretty ordinary. Amenities include tennis courts, 2 beach-side pools, shops, a spa and a Pacific Ocean backdrop.
✉ 1500 Orange Ave, Coronado (8, H3) ☎ 935-435 6611; fax 522 8262 ❸ www.hoteldel.com 🚍 MTS 901, 902, 904, 910 ✕ 3 eateries

J Street Inn $

Very postmodern, rather hip, totally inexpensive and ideally located between the Embarcadero and the Gaslamp Quarter. All units have kitchenettes, some have harbour views.
✉ 222 J St, Gaslamp Quarter (9, E3) ☎ 619-696 6922 🚍 MTS 1, 4, 5 🚊 Orange Line

La Pensione Hotel $

Very clean and well designed, this stylish corner hotel is in the heart of Little Italy. Rooms have basic cooking facilities and there's a laundry and cafe on the premises.
✉ 1700 India St, Little Italy (9, B2) ☎ 619-236 8000; fax 236 8088 ❸ www.sdie.net-lapensione 🚍 MTS 5, 16 🚊 Blue Line ✕ Indigo Grill, Caffe Talia

La Valencia $$$-$$$$

The pink walls, palm trees and sweeping sea views of this Mediterranean-style

beauty have attracted movie stars and millionaires since it opened in the 1920s.
✉ 1132 Prospect St, La Jolla (8, C1) ☎ 858-454 0771; fax 456 3921 ❸ www.lavalencia.com 🚍 MTS 34, 34A, 34B ✕ Mediterranean, Sky Room, Whaling Bar

US Grant Hotel $$-$$$$

The classiest and most historic downtown hotel, it was built in 1910 by Ulysses S Grant Jr, and has housed a host of famous guests, including Albert Einstein and Harry S Truman. Handsomely renovated in the 1980s, it is beautifully appointed with antique-style furnishings.
✉ 326 Broadway, Gaslamp Quarter (9, D4) ☎ 619-232 3121; fax 232 3626 ❸ www.grandheritage.com 🚍 MTS to Broadway 🚊 Orange Line ✕ Grand Grill, The Bar

AROUND CALIFORNIA

BIG SUR (1, G4)
Deetjen's Big Sur Inn $-$$

Visitors love this rustic conglomeration of rooms, redwoods and wisteria along Castro Creek. It's essential to book ahead.
✉ Hwy 1 ☎ 831-667 2377; fax 667 0466 🚍 Monterey Peninsula Transit ✕ Deetjen's Restaurant

Ventana Big Sur $$$$

A stylish yet low-key country inn that has served as a hideaway for a huge stable of Hollywood A-list stars. An aura of serenity and

romance pervades the complex which integrates a Japanese bathhouse, sauna and 2 pools. Rooms have a spa and fireplace.
✉ Hwy 1 ☎ 831-667 2331; fax 667 2419 ❸ www.ventanainn.com 🚍 Monterey Peninsula Transit ✕ Ventana Restaurant

EUREKA (1, B2)
Carter House Inn $$-$$$

The Carter has earned numerous awards for best inn, best restaurant etc. Rates include a fabulous breakfast, plus wine and

nightly hors d'oeuvres.
✉ 301 L St ☎ 707-444 8062; fax 444 8067 ❸ www.carterhouse.com 🚍 Greyhound from SF ✕ Restaurant 301

Eureka Inn $$

The luxurious Tudor-style Eureka Inn is on the National Register of Historic Places and has every amenity, including a swimming pool, sauna and hot tub, fine restaurants, a pub and 100 rooms.
✉ 518 7th St ☎ 707-442 6441; fax 442 0637 ❸ www.eurekainn.com

🚌 Greyhound from SF
🍴 Rib Room, Bristol
Rose Cafe

MAMMOTH
LAKES   (1, E6)
Shilo Inn $-$$
Sure it's a chain, but it's
hard to beat for comfort
and amenities – fireplace,
microwave, fridge, free continental breakfast, gym
with indoor pool, spa,
steam room and sauna.
✉ 2963 Main St ☎
760-934 4500; fax 934
7594 🌐 www.shiloinns.
com/California/mammo
th_lakes.html 🚌 Grey-
hound from LA 🍴
Chart House

Snow Goose Inn   S
This B&B pampers guests
with lavish breakfasts and
evening appetisers and has
an outdoor spa.
✉ 57 Forest Trail ☎
760-934 2660; fax 934
5655 🌐 www.snowgo
ose-inn.com 🚌 Grey-
hound from LA

MENDOCINO
(1, D2)
**Mendocino
Hotel $-$$$**
Built in 1878 overlooking
the sea, this historic place
has charming rooms, an
elegant Victorian dining
room and a more casual
garden bar and cafe.
✉ 45080 Main St ☎
707-937 0511; fax 937
0513 🌐 www.mendoci
nohotel.com 🍴 Victor-
ian Dining Room,
Garden Room Bar

MONTEREY
PENINSULA (1, F4)
**Candle Light
Inn $$-$$$**
Central and friendly, this
place has snug rooms
equipped with coffee-

makers. The French owner
is a treasure trove of infor-
mation on local restau-
rants. Breakfast is included.
✉ San Carlos St,
Carmel ☎ 760-325
0046; fax 325 0710 🚌
Greyhound from LA & SF

El Adobe Inn $-$$
A well-kept, charming place
a short stroll south of
Monterey. Rates include
breakfast and use of the spa.
✉ 936 Munras Ave,
Monterey ☎ 831-372
5409; fax 624 2967 🚌
Greyhound from LA & SF

Monterey Hotel $$$
Housed in a historic build-
ing in the heart of Old
Monterey, rooms have a
comfortable old-world
charm. A satisfying conti-
nental breakfast is included.
✉ 406 Alvarado St,
Monterey ☎ 831-375
3184; fax 373 2899 🌐
www.montereyhotel.c
om 🚌 Greyhound from
LA & SF

PALM
SPRINGS   (1, J8)
Ingleside Inn $-$$$
A venerable, classy Palm
Springs institution in the
shadow of the San Jacinto
mountains and only 2
blocks from the action of
Palm Canyon Dr.
✉ 200 W Ramon Rd
☎ 760-325 0046; fax
325 0710 🚌 Grey-
hound from LA & San

Diego 🍴 Melvyn's

**Marriott's Desert
Springs Resort
& Spa $$$$**
Launches take you across
an artificial lake to the
restaurant, golf balls whiz
by in the distance and spa
treatments are a common
conversation topic; rates
drop by half in summer.
✉ 74855 Country Club
Drive, Desert Springs
☎ 760-341 2211; fax
341 1872 🌐 marriotth
otels.com/CTDCA 🚌
Greyhound from LA &
San Diego 🍴 4 eateries

**La Mancha
Resort $$-$$$$**
There's no shortage of lux-
ury in Palm Springs and
this place prides itself on
absolute discretion. Book a
room and they won't
breathe a word to anyone.
✉ 444 Avenida
Caballeros ☎ 760-323
1773; fax 323 5928 🌐
www.la-mancha.com
🚌 Greyhound from LA
& San Diego 🍴 Don
Quixote Dining Room

SACRAMENTO
(1, D4)
**Hyatt Regency
Sacramento $$$**
Across from the capitol and
convention centre, the
hotel caters to business
guests. Amenities include a
pool, spa, fitness centre
and 2 restaurants.

On the Cheap
If you're looking for budget lodgings, the cheapest
option is a bunk in a hostel – generally communal
affairs with 4 to 8-bed dorms, shared washrooms
and kitchen. Some hostels also have private rooms,
costing about the same as those at motels and
cheaper hotels.

✉ 1209 L St ☎ 916-443 1234; fax 321 6699 🌐 www.hyatt.com 🚃 Amtrak from LA, SF & San Diego 🚌 Greyhound from LA & SF ✕ Dawson's Steak House, Ciao Yama

SAN LUIS OBISPO (1, G5)
Garden Street Inn $-$$
A lovely B&B with 13 rooms and a central location. Perks include a really big breakfast, and wine and cheese on arrival.
✉ 1212 Garden St ☎ 805-545 9802; fax 545 9013 🌐 www.fix.net\garden 🚃 Amtrak from LA & SF 🚌 Greyhound from LA & SF

Madonna Inn $-$$
Over-the-top, eccentric, tacky – this is a landmark in the upper stratosphere of bad taste. Choose from 109 themed rooms, including the Caveman Room (carved from solid rock) or the Austrian Room with crystal chandeliers and baroque furniture. Don't miss the singing toilets.
✉ Hwy 1/101 ☎ 805-543 3000; fax 543 1800 🌐 www.madonnainn.com 🚃 Amtrak from LA & SF 🚌 Greyhound from LA & SF ✕ Pastry Shop, Coffee Shop, Gold Rush Steak House

SANTA BARBARA (1, H5)
El Encanto Hotel & Garden Villas $$$-$$$$
Long considered *the* hotel in Santa Barbara. Secluded cottages with private patios nestle among 10 acres of lush gardens on a hill above the mission with a great view of downtown and the ocean.
✉ 1900 Lasuen Rd ☎ 805-687 5000; fax 687 3903 🌐 www.srf-worldhotels.com 🚃 Amtrak from LA & SF 🚌 Greyhound from LA & SF ✕ El Encanto

Franciscan Inn $
Easily the best deal near the sea, the Franciscan has a pool, spa and guest laundry and is run with efficiency and charm. A generous breakfast is included.
✉ 109 Bath St ☎ 805-963 8845; fax 564 3295 🌐 www.franciscaninn.com 🚃 Amtrak from LA & SF 🚌 Greyhound from LA & SF

WINE COUNTRY (5, A3)
Euro Spa & Inn $$-$$$
Two 90-minute spa packages (mud bath, sauna etc) are included in the Euro's room rates, making this a very good deal for the area.

✉ 1202 Pine St, Calistoga (1, D3) ☎ 707-942 6829; fax 942 1138 🌐 pschreine@earthlink.com; www.eurospa.com 🚌 Napa Valley Transit 10

Mount View Hotel $$
Historic style coupled with modern facilities, mud baths and swimming pools give this hotel a loyal patronage.
✉ 1457 Lincoln Ave, Calistoga (1, D3) ☎ 707-942 6877; fax 942 6904 🚌 Napa Valley Transit 10 ✕ Catahoula Restaurant

Sonoma Mission Inn & Spa $$-$$$
Peacefully pink, this is the perfect spot for an indulgent weekend getaway – from gourmet dining to individual pampering by highly trained spa staff.
✉ 18140 Sonoma Hwy, Sonoma (5, A2) ☎ 707-938 9000; fax 996 5358 🌐 sm@smispa.com; www.sonomamissioninn.com 🚌 Golden Gate Transit 90 ✕ The Grille, The Cafe

White Sulphur Springs Resort $-$$$
California's oldest resort has private cottages, inn rooms and smallish rooms (with shared bath) in the main Carriage House. It's a peaceful place, with hot springs, a swimming pool and a redwood grove.
✉ 3100 White Sulphur Springs Rd, St Helena (1, D3) ☎ 707-963 8588; fax 963 2890 🌐 www.whitesulphursprings.com 🚌 Napa Valley Transit 10

Back to Nature
State park campgrounds cost $7-$11 and include potable water, picnic tables and fire pits; flush toilets and electricity are rare. National park campgrounds ($14) are generally more spiffy, with flush toilets and access to hot showers.

Private campgrounds offer hot showers, laundry facilities, a store and often a pool or volleyball courts.

facts for the visitor

Downhill on Hyde Street, San Francisco

PRE-DEPARTURE

Travel Requirements

Passport
Must be valid for 6 months from date of entry.

Visa
Not required by citizens of the EU, Australia and New Zealand for visits up to 90 days.

Return/Onward Ticket
Required for entry.

Immunisations
May be required if arriving from cholera and yellow fever areas.

Travel Insurance
A policy that covers theft, loss, flight cancellations and medical problems is a must; check with your travel agent.

Driving Permit
Visitors can drive using their home-country driving licence.

Keeping Copies
Photocopy important documents (keep them separate from the originals) and leave a copy at home. You can also store details of documents in Lonely Planet's free online Travel Vault, password-protected and accessible worldwide. See www.ekno.lonelyplanet.com.

Tourist Information Abroad

The US currently has no government-affiliated tourist offices in other countries.

Climate & When to Go

California has a diverse climate, with great variation between the warmer south and the cooler north. San Francisco is famous for its year-round fog, and while the deserts are notorious for their extremely high temperatures, nights can be chilly wherever you are.

Median LA temperatures are around 70°F (21°C), with summer typically mid 80s (28°C) to low 90s (32°C), and winter mid 50s (12°C) to low 60s (15°C). In San Francisco, temperatures range between 55 and 70°F most of the year, with above 80°F days occurring now and then from spring to autumn.

The best times to visit are April to early June and September and October, when there's some brilliant weather and you'll miss most of the tourist rush. Try to avoid the summer school holiday period (early June to early September).

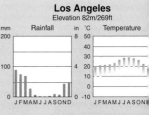

Los Angeles
Elevation 82m/269ft

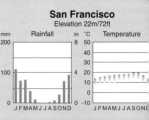

San Francisco
Elevation 22m/72ft

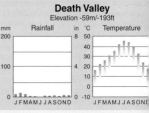

Death Valley
Elevation -59m/-193ft

ARRIVAL & DEPARTURE

The main gateway airports are Los Angeles (LAX) and San Francisco (SFO). Domestic flights touch down at many other centres, the busiest being San Diego. California can be reached by direct flights from the UK, Australia, New Zealand and South Africa. High season is mid-June to mid-September and the week either side of Christmas. The best fares are available from November to March.

Excellent highways connect California with the rest of North America, and train and bus services are quite good. By car it's about 3hrs from LA to Las Vegas, 4hrs from San Francisco to Reno and 17hrs from San Francisco to Seattle.

Air

LAX, 17 miles south-west of Downtown LA, has 8 terminals. Most international carriers land at the Tom Bradley terminal, though larger US airlines such as United and TWA have their own terminals, with free shuttles. Mid-sized LA area airports for domestic travel are in Burbank, Ontario/San Bernardino County, Long Beach and Irvine/Orange County.

Most international flights to the Bay Area land at the International Terminal of SFO, 14 miles south of downtown on the west side of the bay. Oakland and San Jose are important domestic gateways.

Information
General Inquiries LAX ☎ 310-646 5252, www.lawa.org; SFO ☎ 650-876 7809, www.sfoairport.com

Flight Information Contact the airline: American ☎ 800-433 7300; British Airways ☎ 800-247 9297; Qantas Airways ☎ 800-227 4500; South African Airways ☎ 800-722 9675; United ☎ 800-241 6522; Virgin Atlantic ☎ 800-862 8621.

Carpark Information LAX ☎ 310-646 9070; SFO ☎ 650-877 0227

Left Luggage All LAX and SFO terminals have lockers in the boarding areas. At LAX, larger items can be stored in terminals 1, 3, 7 and Tom Bradley.

Airport Access
Bus Shuttles run a 24hr service between LAX and hotels in the LA and Orange County areas (usually $10-$20). They include Prime Time (☎ 800-262 7433) and Super Shuttle (☎ 800-258 3826).

Shuttles from SFO cost $9-$12 one way, or $16 round-trip, and include the American Airporter (☎ 415-546 6689), Super Shuttle (☎ 415 558 8500) and Lorrie's (☎ 415-334 9000). Airport transport buses include the SFO Airporter (☎ 415-495 8404) and the Bay Area Shuttle (☎ 650-873 7771), servicing major East Bay hotels ($22-$24 one way).

Taxi LAX to Santa Monica $25; Downtown or Hollywood $35; Anaheim $80. SFO to downtown $25-$35.

Train Neither LAX nor SFO is directly served by rail. Aviation (Metro Green Line) is the closest station to LAX, reached by a free 10-minute shuttle bus. From SFO, Sam Trans express bus No 3X takes 20 minutes to reach the Colma BART station for downtown, the East Bay or Oakland.

Train

In LA, trains arrive and depart from Union Station (3, D4), 800 N Alameda St, Downtown. The nearest Amtrak terminal in San

Francisco is at Jack London Square in Oakland.

For information and bookings in LA call ☎ 213-624 0171; in San Francisco call ☎ 800-872 7245.

See www.amtrak.com for arrival/departure times.

Bus

Greyhound's 24hr main LA terminal (☎ 213-629 8421) is at 1716 E 7th St, Downtown (2, D5). In San Francisco, all bus services use the Transbay Terminal (☎ 415-495 1575), 425 Mission St (7, C5).

Customs

Amounts in excess of $10,000 in cash, travellers cheques, money orders et must be declared. As California is a important agricultural state, mos food products must also be declarec

There are 2 colour-coded cus toms channels: green (nothing to declare) and red (something to declare).

Duty Free

Travellers over the age of 21 ca import 1L of liquor and 200 ciga rettes. US citizens can import $40(worth of gifts from abroad; non-U citizens $100 worth.

Departure Tax

Departure tax ($6) is included in the price of your ticket.

GETTING AROUND

The best way to see California is by car. The exception is San Francisco, where parking can be difficult and public transport is excellent. San Diego has a good public bus and trolley system, but it only runs to around 6.30pm. You *can* get around LA by bus, but the system is limited.

It's worth flying between major hubs, as bus and train schedules are often inconvenient and fares are relatively high.

Travel Passes

Air Passes
Almost all domestic carriers offer Visit USA passes to non-US citizens. The passes are actually a book of coupons – each coupon equals a flight. They must be purchased with an international airline ticket anywhere outside the USA except Canada or Mexico. Coupons cost $100-$160, depending on how many you buy.

Most airlines require you to plar your itinerary and to complete your flights within 60 days o arrival in the US. A few airlines may allow you to call a day or so before the flight and make a 'standby reservation'.

Train Passes
Amtrak's Explore America Pass per mits 3 stops within 45 days of trav el ($179 for one region). Non-U' citizens also have the option of the USA Rail Pass which allows trav ellers to get on and off wherever they wish within its life span (1! days West Coast $315 high season $195 low season).

Bus Passes
Greyhound's Ameripass (only avail able outside the USA) gives unlim ited bus travel for 7 ($199), 1! ($299) and 30 ($409) days.

Local Transport Passes

The San Francisco Muni Passport, available for 1, 3 or 7 days, allows unlimited travel on all Muni transport, including cable cars. The San Diego Day Tripper Transit Pass offers unlimited travel on local buses, the trolley and the bay ferry.

Air

Internal flights are a convenient way of getting around, and if you take advantage of airline deals it can work out not much more expensive than travelling by bus, train or rental car. A number of routes have especially frequent and convenient services, including San Francisco-Los Angeles (SF-LA), SF-Burbank, SF-Orange County, SF-San Diego, SF-Reno, Oakland-LA and LA-Las Vegas. On these routes it's often possible to go to the airport, buy a ticket and hop aboard.

Train

Statewide

Amtrak (☎ 800-872 7245, 800-USA-RAIL) is the national rail system, servicing major US cities. The trains are comfortable, with dining and lounge cars on long-distance routes. Reservations can be made up to 11 months in advance. Four main routes operate within California: the *San Joaquin* route from Oakland/Emeryville to Los Angeles; the *San Diegan* from San Luis Obispo to San Diego; the *Three Capitals* between Sacramento and San Jose; and the *Coast Starlight* between Seattle, Oakland, San Jose and LA. Amtrak Thruway buses connect to rural towns and Yosemite National Park.

CalTrain (☎ 800-660 4287) links SF with San Jose and Palo Alto; the depot is at the corner of 4th and Townsend Sts (6, C3).

Los Angeles

Los Angeles' Metro Rail (☎ 213-626 4455) operates 3 light-rail lines connecting Downtown with Hollywood, Long Beach, Redondo Beach and Norwalk ($1.35 one way). Metrolink (☎ 800-371 5465) extends further afield to Orange, Riverside, San Bernardino and Ventura counties.

San Francisco

San Francisco's Bay Area Rapid Transit (BART; ☎ 650-992 2278) subway system links the city with the Bay Area ($1.10 to $4.70). Services operate from 4am (Sat 6am, Sun 8am) to 11pm or midnight, and tickets can be bought from vending machines.

Bus

Greyhound (☎ 800-231 2222; www.greyhound.com) has extensive scheduled routes and its own terminal in most cities. Green Tortoise buses (☎ 800-867 8647; www.greentortoise.com) provide sleeping bunks; they travel Hwy 1 between LA and SF ($35).

Los Angeles

In LA, a network of 208 separate bus routes spans the metropolis, the majority operated by the Metropolitan Transport Authority (MTA; ☎ 800-266 6883). The base fare is $1.35 (have exact change), and most services run from 5am-2am. Customer centres can be found at Union Station (3, D4); the ARCO Plaza, LC, 515 S Flower St (3, G2); and 5301 Wilshire Blvd (4, D4).

Downtown Area Short Hop

LA's DASH minibuses run every 6-15 minutes between Downtown's most interesting areas from 6.30am to 6.30pm weekdays, 10am-5pm on Saturday. The DASH routes service

Chinatown, Little Tokyo, Exposition Park, Central Library and the Arts District; 25c per trip.

Useful Bus Routes

Hollywood Blvd	1
Sunset Blvd	2
Santa Monica Blvd	4
Melrose Ave	10
Wilshire Blvd	20
Beverly Hills	27
Venice Beach	33
Long Beach	60
Burbank Studios	96
Disneyland	460

San Francisco

The San Francisco Municipal Railway (☎ 415-673 6864), known as Muni, operates the city's bus lines, streetcars and cable cars ($1 standard fare). A Visitor Information Center is at Hallidie Plaza, on the corner of Market and Powell Sts (7, D4). A limited 'Owl' service runs from 1-5am.

Useful Bus Routes

Fulton	5
Haight	7
Mission	14
3rd St	15
Fillmore	22
Valencia	26
19th Ave	28
Embarcadero	32

Streetcar & Cable Car

San Francisco's streetcars and cable cars are operated by Muni ($1 standard fare).

Antique streetcars from around the world run on the F-Market above-ground line, while the remaining lines run mostly underground. Most streetcars operate from 5 or 6am to midnight.

San Francisco's cable cars are mainly used by tourists and run on 3 routes – California St, Powell-Mason Sts and Powell-Hyde Sts. The standard fare is $2, and an all day ticket costs $6; the cars operate from around 6am-12.30am.

In San Diego, trolleys run from the terminal near the Santa Fe Depot, and are operated by the Metropolitan Transit Service (MTS; ☎ 619-233 3004).

Taxi

Taxis are metered, with charges from $2 at flag fall, plus $1.80 per mile (plus 50c per piece of luggage).

In LA try Checker (☎ 323-481 2345) or United Independent (☎ 310-278 2500); in SF try City Cab (☎ 415-468 7200) or Yellow Cab (☎ 415-626 2345); in San Diego try American Cab (☎ 619-292 1111) or Silver Cab (☎ 619-280 5555).

Boat

Ferries operate from Long Beach and LA Harbor to Santa Catalina Island. On San Francisco Bay there's Blue & Gold's Alameda Oakland Ferry (☎ 510-522 3300), as well as those going to Alcatraz and Angel Island (☎ 415-705 5555), and Vallejo (☎ 415-705 5444). Golden Gate Ferries (☎ 415-923 2000) operate to Larkspur and Sausalito.

Car & Motorcycle

Driving is the easiest, cheapest way to get around (except in downtown San Francisco). For road conditions anywhere in California call ☎ 800-427 7623.

Road Rules

Vehicles drive on the right-hand side of the road; seat belts must be worn and children must have proper seats and restraints; motorcyclists must wear helmets.

Speed Limits The limit is 65 or 75mph on interstates and freeways; 55mph or less on other highways; from 25 to 45mph in cities.

Drink-Driving A blood alcohol concentration of 0.08% or more (0.01% if you are under 21 years old) could lead to a jail sentence of 48 hours to 6 months, $390 to $1000 in fines and suspension of your licence for up to a year.

Car Rental
The major nationwide car rental companies include Avis (☎ 800-831 2847), Budget (800-527 0700), Dollar (☎ 800-800 4000), Hertz (☎ 800-654 3131), National (☎ 800-328 4567) and Thrifty (☎ 800-367 2277). Rates range from $25-$45 per day, $120-$200 per week. Basic unleaded petrol costs around $1.20 per gallon.

Motoring Organisations
The American Automobile Association (AAA; ☎ 800-222 4357, 800-AAA HELP) has offices in all major cities and many smaller towns, and provides emergency roadside service. The AAA has reciprocal arrangements with similar organisations overseas.

PRACTICAL INFORMATION
Tourist Information

California Office of Tourism
(☎ 800-862 2543; www.gocalif.ca.gov) 801 K St, suite 1600, Sacramento, CA 95814; they will send you out a wad of brochures and maps on request

Hollywood Visitor Information Center
(☎ 323-236 2331) 6541 Hollywood Blvd, LA (4, B2); specialises in Tinseltown

LA Convention & Visitors Bureau
(☎ 323-689 8822) 685 S Figueroa St (3, G2); has a 24hr multilingual events hotline (☎ 213-689 8822)

Monterey Chamber of Commerce Visitors Center
(☎ 831-649 1770) Camino El Estero & Franklin; has direct-dial phones to more than 40 hotels

Palm Springs Visitor Center
(☎ 760-778 8418) 2781 N Palm Canyon Dr; open year-round, books accommodation, desert tours and golf packages

Sacramento Visitor Information Center
(☎ 916-442 7644) 1101 2nd St, Old Sacramento; recommends accommodation and has free city maps

San Diego International Visitors Information Center
(☎ 619-236 1212) 1st Ave (9, E3); stocks discount coupons for the city's major sights

San Francisco Visitor Information Center
(☎ 415-391 2000) Hallidie Plaza, cnr Market & Powell Sts (7, D4); has lots of practical information and a 'what's on' infoline (☎ 415-391 2001)

Consulates

Most foreign embassies are in Washington, DC, but the following countries have consular offices in California:

Los Angeles
Australia	(☎ 323-469 4300)
Canada	(☎ 323-346 2700)
Japan	(☎ 213-617 6700)
New Zealand	(☎ 310-207 1605)
UK	(☎ 310-477 3322)

San Francisco
Australia	(☎ 415-362 6160)

Canada	(☎ 415-543 2550)
Japan	(☎ 415-777 3533)
New Zealand	(☎ 415-399 1455)
UK	(☎ 415-981 3030)

Money

Currency

The unit of currency is the US dollar, divided into 100 cents.

Coins are 1c (penny), 5c (nickel), 10c (dime), 25c (quarter), and the seldom-seen 50c (half-dollar).

Notes are $1, $2, $5, $10, $20, $50 and $100.

Travellers Cheques

US dollar travellers cheques are accepted by restaurants, hotels and most stores as if they were cash, so you'll never have to exchange them at a bank or pay an exchange fee. American Express (☎ 800-528 4800) and Thomas Cook (☎ 800-287 7362) are widely accepted and have efficient replacement policies.

Credit Cards

All major credit cards are widely accepted. For lost cards contact:

American Express	☎ 800-528 4800
Diners Club	☎ 800-234 6377
Discover	☎ 800-347 2683
MasterCard	☎ 800-826 2181
Visa	☎ 800-336 8472

Changing Money

Most major currencies and leading brands of travellers cheques are easily exchanged at banks, which usually offer the best rates.

Tipping

Cloakroom attendants	50c-$1
Guides	$1-$5 per person
Hairdressers	15%
Porters	$1 for the first bag, 50c for each additional bag
Restaurants	15%

Room cleaners	$1 per person
Taxis	10%
Theater ushers	$1
Restroom attendants	50c

Concessions

Student & Youth Cards

ISIC or university ID cards can provide discounts on theatre tickets museum entrance fees, transport passes and theme park entry.

Senior Citizens

People aged 50 years and over can receive discounts at hotels, museums and restaurants. All you need is an ID with photograph and proof of age.

Automobile Association Cards

AAA discounts on accommodation can be claimed by members of affiliated groups.

Opening Hours

Banks
   Mon-Fri 9am-5pm; some also open Sat 9am-2pm

Post Offices
   Mon-Fri 9am-5pm

Offices
   Mon-Fri 9am-5pm

Shops
   Mon-Sat 9/10am to 5/6pm; often until 9pm in malls; Sun 12-5pm

Pharmacies
   24hrs

Tourist Sites
   10am-6pm, some until midnight in summer

Public Holidays

New Year's Day	1 Jan
Martin Luther King Day	Jan (3rd Mon)
Presidents' Day	Feb (3rd Mon)
Easter Monday	Mar/Apr
Memorial Day	May (last Mon)

Independence Day	4 Jul
Labor Day	Sep (1st Mon)
Columbus Day	Oct (2nd Mon)
Veterans Day	11 Nov
Thanksgiving	Nov (4th Thurs)
Christmas Day	25 Dec

Banks, schools and government offices (including post offices) are closed and transport, museums and other services run on a Sunday schedule. Individual businesses, museums and restaurants may close, particularly on Thanksgiving, Christmas and New Year's Day. Many holidays are observed on the closest Monday.

Time

Pacific Standard Time is 8hrs behind GMT, and 3hrs behind EST. During Daylight Saving Time (first Sunday in April to last Saturday in October) the clock is moved forward 1hr.

At noon in California, it is:

3pm in New York
8pm in London
9pm in Paris
10pm in Cape Town
6am (the next day) in Sydney

Electricity

Standard voltage throughout the USA is 110 volts and 60Hz. Plugs have 2 (flat) or 3 (2 flat, 1 round) pins and adapters are widely available.

Weights & Measures

Distances are in feet, yards and miles, and dry weights are in ounces, pounds and tons. Gasoline (petrol) is dispensed by the US gallon which, along with US pints and quarts, is about 20% less than the Imperial measurement. See the conversion table on page 121.

Post

The US Postal Service (USPS; ☎ 800-275 8777, www.usps.gov.) is reliable and inexpensive. Every incorporated town has a post office, even if it's closet-sized. Larger cities have a central post office, plus smaller branches. Most offices have a stamp vending machine, and you can buy stamps at supermarkets and drugstores.

LA's main post office (☎ 213-617 4543) is near Union Station at 900 N Alameda St (3, C4). San Francisco's (☎ 800-725 2161) is at Civic Center, 101 Hyde St (7, E4).

Postal Rates

Rates for letters sent 1st class within the US are 33c. Postcards are 20c.

Airmail rates are 60c for a half-ounce letter, $1 for a 1oz letter and 40c for each additional half ounce. International postcard rates are 50c. For heavier items, rates differ according to the distance mailed. Books, periodicals and computer disks can be sent by a cheaper 4th class rate.

Telephone

Public payphones are either coin or card-operated; some also accept credit cards. Local calls usually cost a minimum of 35c and increase with distance and length of call.

Phonecards

Phonecards are available from retail outlets and vending machines and come in $5, $10, $20 and $50 denominations.

Lonely Planet's eKno Communication Card provides competitive international calls (avoid using it for local calls), messaging services and free email. For free information on joining and accessing the service, see the eKno site at www.ekno.lonelyplanet.com.

Useful Numbers

Operator	☎ 0
Local Directory Inquiries	☎ 411
Int'l Dialling Code	☎ 011
MCI	☎ 1800-888 8000
AT&T	☎ 1800-225 5288

International Codes

Australia	☎ 61
Japan	☎ 81
New Zealand	☎ 64
South Africa	☎ 27
UK	☎ 44

Email/www

You can log on to the Net at most public libraries or at Internet cafes. Major Internet service providers such as AOL (www.aol.com), CompuServe (www.compuserve.com) and IBM Net (www.ibm.net) have dial-in nodes throughout the US.

Useful Sites

Lonely Planet's Web site (www.lonelyplanet.com) provides destination info, travel news, travellers' tips and links to useful travel resources. Most tourist offices and travel organisations maintain useful sights. Others to try include:

Business Travel
  www.thetrip.com

California Division of Tourism
  www.gocalif.ca.gov

California State Automobile Association Travel Service
  www.csaa.com/travel

Hotels & Resorts in the US
  www.hotelstravel.com/us.html

US Cities
  www.usacitylink.com

Internet Cafes

Los Angeles

World Cafe
  (☎ 310-392 1661) 2820 Main St, Santa Monica (2, D1)

Cyber Java
  (☎ 323-466 5600) 7080 Hollywood Blvd (4, C1); open 24hrs

San Francisco

Yakety Yak
  (☎ 415- 885 6908) 679 Sutter St, Union Square (7, D4)

Muddy Waters Coffeehouse
  (☎ 415-621 2233) 260 Church St, The Castro (7, H4)

Doing Business

LA is the largest business, financial and industrial centre on the West Coast, and has a host of advocacy and outreach programs. The Los Angeles Economic Development Corporation (LAEDC, ☎ 213-622 4300; www.laedc.org), 515 S Flower St, Downtown (3, G2), can provide a good overview.

Newspapers & Magazines

Broadsheet newspapers include the *LA Times*, *San Francisco Chronicle* and *San Diego Union*.

Local magazines worth checking out include *LA Business Journal* and *Los Angeles Magazine*.

Especially good for events listings are the free street papers *SF Weekly*, *Bay Guardian*, *LA Weekly* and *San Diego Reader*.

Radio

Los Angeles

KCRW (89.9 FM)	Public radio
KUSC (91.5 FM)	Classical music
KIIS (102.7 FM)	Top 40
STAR (98.7 FM)	Alternative pop

San Francisco

KQED (88.5 FM)	Public radio
KPFA (94.1 FM	News and music
KDFC (102.1 FM)	Classical
KITS (105.3 FM)	Alternative rock

TV

In LA, the major network affiliates are KCBS (2), KNBC (4), KABC (7) and KTTV-Fox (11), with independent stations KTLA (5) and KCOP (13); KCET (28) is the Public Broadcasting System (PBS) affiliate. Cable stations include CNN (news), ESPN (sports), HBO (movies) and MTV (music). In San Francisco local programming can be found on KQED (9), the PBS affiliate, and TV-20 is quirky.

Photography & Video

Print film is widely available at supermarkets and discount drugstores. Slide film can be bought in larger stores, photography shops and around major tourist attractions. Film is susceptible to heat, so protect your film by keeping it cool and processing it as soon as possible.

The USA uses the National Television System Committee (NTSC) colour TV standard, which is not compatible with video standards used in Africa, Europe, Asia and Australia (PAL or SECAM), unless converted.

Health

Precautions

In LA especially, it's best to wear plenty of sunscreen. Take time to acclimatise to high temperatures and make sure you drink sufficient liquids. Tap water is fine to drink.

Insurance & Medical Treatment

Because of the high cost of health care, international travellers should take out comprehensive travel insurance. Emergency rooms are incredibly expensive; try hospital 'urgent care clinics' for less serious injuries and illnesses.

Medical Services

The following hospitals have 24hr urgent care clinics:

Los Angeles

Hollywood Presbyterian Medical Center (☎ 323-660 5350) 1300 N Vermont Ave, Hollywood (2, C4)

Cedars-Sinai Medical Center (☎ 310-855 5000) 8700 Beverly Blvd, Beverly Hills (4, G3)

San Francisco

San Francisco General Hospital (☎ 415-206 8000) 1001 Potrero Ave, The Mission (6, D5)

San Diego

Mercy Hospital (☎ 619-294 8111) 4077 5th Ave, Mission Hills (8, F4)

Mission Bay Hospital (☎ 619-274-7721) 3030 Bunker Hill St, Pacific Beach (8, D2)

Dental Emergencies

In San Francisco contact the Dental Information Service (☎ 415-398 0618). In other cities, look under 'Dentists' in the Yellow Pages.

Pharmacies & Drugs

Longs, Sav-On, Rite Aid and Walgreens are chain-owned pharmacies that open 24hrs; look in the White Pages for the nearest one.

HIV/AIDS

AIDS support groups are listed in the front of phone books; the AIDS Hotline is ☎ 800-342 2437 nationwide.

HIV/AIDS is viewed as a communicable disease and is grounds for exclusion from the US. For more information, contact the Immigrant HIV Assistance Project, Bar Association of San Francisco (☎ 415-267 0795), 685 Market St, Suite 700, San Francisco, CA 94105.

Emergency Numbers

Ambulance, police & fire
☎ 911 (LA & SF)

Suicide prevention
☎ 800-333 444 (LA)
☎ 415-781 0500 (SF)

Crisis Response Unit
☎ 800-833 3376 (LA)

Rape Crisis Hotline
☎ 310-392 8381 (LA)
☎ 415-647 7273 (SF)

Toilets

Public toilets are usually free and clean. If there is no public toilet around when you need one, ask at a gas station, restaurant or bar – people are usually very accommodating (especially to women).

Safety Concerns

Road accidents are probably the greatest single risk of injury; otherwise, California is not a dangerous place, but there are some things to beware of. There is some risk of violent crime, but it is mostly confined to well-defined areas, notably in parts of Oakland, South San Francisco, Bakersfield, Modesto and Stockton, and parts of LA such as Compton, Watts and South Central. Avoid these neighbourhoods, especially after dark. Car theft and car jackings are more common in LA than in other parts of the country. Then there's earthquakes, where the main danger is being hit by something falling.

Lost Property
Theme parks, museums, airports and hotels have 'Lost & Found' departments where your goods may turn up.

Women Travellers

California is a liberated state, but women should be careful when walking anywhere alone after dark. Places to be especially careful are parking structures, bus and train stations, public parks and small rural towns where solo women travellers don't often venture. In large urban centres, smaller towns with college or university students, and national parks, you can expect little, if any, reaction if you're a woman travelling alone. Given strict US sexual harassment laws, getting hassled by men is much rarer in California than in other parts of the world.

The contraceptive pill is available by prescription only, so a visit to the doctor is necessary. Tampons are available from drugstores (chemists) and supermarkets.

Organisations
The California chapter of the National Organization of Women (NOW) has a good Web site (www.canow.org). Some of the major women's organisations are:

Los Angeles
Women Helping Women Services talkline
(☎ 213-655 3807)

YWCA
(☎ 213-295 4288) 2501 W Vernon Ave
(☎ 310-452 3881) 2019 14th St, Santa Monica

San Francisco
Women's Building
(☎ 415-431 1180) 3543 18th St

St Luke's Women's Center
(☎ 415-285 7788) 1650 Valencia St

Gay & Lesbian Travellers

The most established gay communities are in major cities, where gay men and women can live their lives openly. With the nation's largest gay population residing in San Francisco, Californians have become tolerant in all but the smallest towns.

Along with The Castro district of San Francisco, there are established gay communities in Hillcrest, San Diego, in West Hollywood and in Palm Springs/Cathedral City.

In California, homosexual sex is legal over the age of 18.

Information & Organisations

Check the Yellow Pages under 'Gay & Lesbian Organizations' for listings of community resources. The LA Gay & Lesbian Center (☎ 323-993 7400), 1625 N Schrader Blvd, West Hollywood, is a one-stop service and health agency. The Gay, Lesbian & Bi Center (☎ 310-379 2850) is at 2009a Artesia Blvd in Redondo Beach. Useful numbers include San Francisco's Gay, Lesbian, Bisexual & Transgender Switchboard Hotline (☎ 510-841 6224) and the Gay Youth Talk Line (☎ 800-246 7743).

Useful listings magazines include *Frontiers, Edge, In Los Angeles, Front, Lesbian News* and *LA Girl Guide*, while *Betty & Pansy's Severe Queer Review of San Francisco* is a must.

Senior Travellers

For information on recreational and other activities contact local seniors centres (see the Yellow Pages), the Los Angeles Area Agency on Aging (☎ 213-738 4004) or the American Association of Retired Persons (AARP; ☎ 800-424 3410, www.aarp.org), 3200 E Carson St, Lakewood, CA 90712.

Disabled Travellers

Thanks to the Americans with Disabilities Act (ADA), all public buildings (including hotels, restau-

rants, theatres and museums) must be wheelchair accessible, buses and trains must have wheelchair lifts (they also allow service animals and sell 2-for-1 packages when attendants are required) and telephone companies are required to provide relay operators for the hearing impaired. Many banks now provide ATM instructions in braille and you will find audible crossing signals as well as dropped curbs at most intersections.

Larger private and chain hotels have suites for disabled guests, with Hilton, Hyatt and Embassy Suites being the most reliable. Car rental agencies such as Budget, Hertz and Enterprise offer hand-controlled vehicles and vans with wheelchair lifts at no extra charge (reserve well in advance). Wheelers (☎ 800-456 1371), a subdivision of Avis, specialises in such vehicles.

Parking

Disabled parking is permitted on blue-coloured curbs (ID required).

Information & Organisations

For MTA information on LA's wheelchair-accessible bus schedules call ☎ 213-626 4455. All Bay Area transit companies offer travel discounts for the disabled, and all Muni Metro and BART stations are wheelchair accessible. Also check the following:

Center for Independent Living
(☎ 510-841 4776) Telegraph Ave, Berkeley, CA 94705; provides counselling and information services

Travel Industry Disabled Exchange
(☎ 818-343 6339) 5435 Donna Ave, Tarzana, CA 91356; subscription news and information service

Society for the Advancement of Travel for the Handicapped
(☎ 212-447 7284; sathtravel@aol.com) 347 Fifth Ave No 610, New York, NY 10016

Language

The movie *Blade Runner*, set in LA, featured an early 21st-century street-pidgin of Spanish, English, German and Japanese that's not so far-fetched. Common usage of foreign words goes almost totally unnoticed; for example, Spanish (*canyon*, *rodeo*, *rancho*, *playa*); Native American (*moccasin*, *kayak*, *toboggan*); German (*kindergarten*, *loafer*, *hoodlum*); and Yiddish (*kitsch*, *schmuck*, *schmaltz*).

According to a 1997 census, around 42% of Californians over 5 years old speak a language other than English at home. Los Angeles, San Francisco and most San Joaquin Valley towns have neighborhoods where Spanish, Chinese, Japanese, Vietnamese, Korean, or Cambodian is the dominant language. Still, American English predominates on the streets and in places of business.

California's most recognised dialect, the style presented in songs and movies, comes from the beaches and shopping malls of Southern California. This casual talk is usually called 'surfer' or 'valley' talk (as in San Fernando Valley), though the two are very similar.

So-Cal Lingo

Some common Californian slang words you might encounter include:

killer, bitchin', awesome, sweet, stylin', stellar – really good

bunk, nappy, shitty, slack – really bad

hairy – scary

gnarly, insane – anything extreme

totally, hella – placed before a word to make its meaning more significant

vibes – feelings or indications you get from a person or place

dude – can be male or female, and is often preceded by *hey*, the common term for 'hi'

cruise – to go (by foot, car, bike or skateboard)

alright, right on – confirmation that you and whoever you're speaking with are *on the same wavelength* (have similar understanding)

The murals which line the back fences and garage doors of San Francisco's Balmy Alley reflect the Latino experience of the past 30 years.

Conversion Table

Clothing Sizes

Measurements approximate only; try before you buy.

Women's Clothing

Aust/NZ	8	10	12	14	16	18
Europe	36	38	40	42	44	46
Japan	5	7	9	11	13	15
UK	8	10	12	14	16	18
USA	6	8	10	12	14	16

Women's Shoes

Aust/NZ	5	6	7	8	9	10
Europe	35	36	37	38	39	40
France only	35	36	38	39	40	42
Japan	22	23	24	25	26	27
UK	3½	4½	5½	6½	7½	8½
USA	5	6	7	8	9	10

Men's Clothing

Aust/NZ	92	96	100	104	108	112
Europe	46	48	50	52	54	56
Japan	S		M	M		L
UK	35	36	37	38	39	40
USA	35	36	37	38	39	40

Men's Shirts (Collar Sizes)

Aust/NZ	38	39	40	41	42	43
Europe	38	39	40	41	42	43
Japan	38	39	40	41	42	43
UK	15	15½	16	16½	17	17½
USA	15	15½	16	16½	17	17½

Men's Shoes

Aust/NZ	7	8	9	10	11	12
Europe	41	42	43	44½	46	47
Japan	26	27	27.5	28	29	30
UK	7	8	9	10	11	12
USA	7½	8½	9½	10½	11½	12½

Weights & Measures

Length & Distance

1 inch = 2.54cm
1cm = 0.39 inches
1m = 3.3ft
1ft = 0.3m
1km = 0.62 miles
1 mile = 1.6km

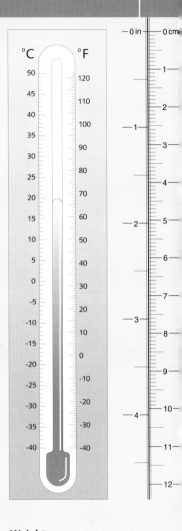

Weight

1kg = 2.2lb
1lb = 0.45kg
1g = 0.04oz
1oz = 28g

Volume

1 litre = 0.26 US gallons
1 US gallon = 3.8 litres
1 litre = 0.22 imperial gallons
1 imperial gallon = 4.55 litres

THE AUTHOR

Marisa Gierlich

Thanks to adventurous parents, Marisa started her travels at a young age. She continued travelling on her own as a student at UC Berkeley, making last-minute frenzied calls to her mom ('I'm taking a midnight flight to Istanbul – don't be worried'... click) and communing with bears on Kodiak Island, Alaska. She's hiked most of the western USA, trekked in the Nepal Himalayas, travelled hut-to-hut in the Swiss Alps and climbed Mont Blanc in between fine dining and wine-tasting seminars. If she's not running, surfing or hiking, she's probably cooking, reading about mountaineering or listening to Ravi Shankar with husband Paul in La Jolla, California. She's proud to be an *Angelena*, a native of LA, and will defend her home town against any bad press.

ABOUT LONELY PLANET GUIDEBOOKS

The story begins with a classic travel adventure: Tony and Maureen Wheeler's 1972 journey across Europe and Asia to Australia. Useful information about the overland trail did not exist at that time, so Tony and Maureen published the first Lonely Planet guidebook to meet a growing need.

From a kitchen table, then from a tiny office in Melbourne, Australia, Lonely Planet has become the largest independent travel publisher in the world, an international company with offices in Melbourne, Oakland (USA), London (UK) and Paris (France).

Today there are over 400 titles, including travel guides, city maps, cycling guides, first time travel guides, healthy travel guides, travel atlases, diving guides, pictorial books, phrasebooks, restaurant guides, travel literature, walking guides and world food guides.

At Lonely Planet we believe that travellers can make a positive contribution to the countries they visit – if they respect their host communities and spend their money wisely. Since 1986 a percentage of the income from books has been donated to aid projects and human rights campaigns.

ABOUT THE CONDENSED GUIDES

Other Lonely Planet Condensed guides include: *Amsterdam* (due July 2000), *Crete, London, New York City, Paris* and *Sydney*.

ABOUT THIS BOOK

Series developed by Diana Saad • Edited by Emma Miller, with assistance from Janet Austin • Design & layout by Andrew Weatherill • Publishing Manager Mary Neighbour • Cover design by Indra Kilfoyle • Maps by Charles Rawlings-Way • Software engineering by Dan Levin • Thanks to Andrew Tudor, Brett Pascoe, Fiona Croyden, Gabrielle Green, Lara Morcombe, Paul Clifton, Richard I'Anson, Scott McNeely, Simon Bracken, Tim Uden and Trudi Canavan

LONELY PLANET ONLINE

www.lonelyplanet.com or AOL keyword: lp

Lonely Planet's award-winning Web site has insider info on hundreds of destinations from Amsterdam to Zimbabwe, complete with interactive maps and colour photographs. You'll also find the latest travel news, recent reports from travellers on the road, guidebook upgrades and a lively bulletin board where you can meet fellow travellers, swap recommendations and seek advice.

PLANET TALK

Our FREE quarterly printed newsletter is full of tips from travellers and anecdotes from Lonely Planet authors. Every issue is packed with up-to-date travel news and advice, and includes a postcard from Lonely Planet co-founder Tony Wheeler, mail from travellers, a look at life on the road through the eyes of a Lonely Planet author, topical health advice, prizes for the best travel yarn, news about forthcoming Lonely Planet events and a complete list of Lonely Planet books and products.

To join our mailing list, email us at: go@lonelyplanet.co.uk (UK, Europe and Africa residents); info@lonelyplanet.com (North and South America residents); talk2us@lonelyplanet.com.au (the rest of the world); or contact any Lonely Planet office.

COMET

Our FREE monthly email newsletter brings you all the latest travel news, features, interviews, competitions, destination ideas, travellers' tips & tales, Q&As, raging debates and related links. Find out what's new on the Lonely Planet Web site and which books are about to hit the shelves.

Subscribe from your desktop: www.lonelyplanet.com/comet

LONELY PLANET OFFICES

Australia
PO Box 617, Hawthorn, Victoria 3122
☎ 03 9819 1877 fax 03 9819 6459
email: talk2us@lonelyplanet.com.au

USA
150 Linden St, Oakland, CA 94607
☎ 510 893 8555 TOLL FREE: 800 275 8555
fax 510 893 8572
email: info@lonelyplanet.com

UK
10a Spring Place, London NW5 3BH
☎ 020 7428 4800 fax 020 7428 4828
email: go@lonelyplanet.co.uk

France
1 rue du Dahomey, 75011 Paris
☎ 01 55 25 33 00 fax 01 55 25 33 01
email: bip@lonelyplanet.fr
minitel: 3615 lonelyplanet

World Wide Web: www.lonelyplanet.com or AOL keyword: lp
Lonely Planet Images: lpi@lonelyplanet.com.au

index

for map references see also the Sights Index p.128

Abbreviations
LA – Los Angeles
NP – National Park
SB – Santa Barbara
SD – San Diego
SF – San Francisco
SP – State Park

3Com Park (SF) 94
7969 (LA) 88
924 Gilman (SF) 90

A
Aero (LA) 88
Aerospace Museum 14
AIDS, *see* HIV/AIDS
air travel 109, 111
Alcatraz 40
Aloha Sharkeez (LA) 86
American Automobile
   Association 113, 114
Amtrak 111
Andrew Molera SP 15
Angel Island SP 40
Ansel Adams Center 38
antiques 62, 65-6, 68-9
Anza-Borrego Desert SP 43
arts 10-12, 62, 65-6, 68-9
Asian Art Museum (SF) 21
Avalon 28
Avila Adobe (LA) 19

B
B&Bs, *see* places to stay
backpacking 50
Bahia Don Bravo (SD) 78-9
Balboa Park 14
Bamboo (LA) 73
Barneys (LA) 61
bars 86, 90, 95
BART, *see* Bay Area Rapid
   Transit
baseball 94
basketball 94
Bay Area Discovery Museum 49
Bay Area Rapid Transit 111
Beach Blanket Babylon (SF) 89
beach volleyball 94
beaches 33, 41
Belly Up Tavern, The (SD) 95
Berkeley 37, 64, 74-5
Beverly Hills Hotel (LA) 100
Big Sur 15, 80, 104
Biltmore Hotel (LA) 19
Bimbo's 365 Club (SF) 90
Bishop 47
Bitter End, The (SD) 95
Bix (SF) 75
boat travel 112
Bodega Bay 45
books & bookshops 11-12,
   62-3, 66, 69
Bottle Inn, The (LA) 74

Bottom of the Hill (SF) 90
Bradbury Building 34
Brockton Villa (SD) 79
Bunker Hill (LA) 18
bus travel 58, 110, 111-12

C
Cable Car Barn &
   Powerhouse 38
cable cars 112
Cabrillo National Monument 42
Cafe du Nord (SF) 90-91
Cafe LuLu (SD) 79
Cafe Sevilla (SD) 95
Cafe, The (SF) 93
cafes, *see* places to eat
Caffé Macaroni (SF) 75
California Academy of
   Sciences (SF) 21
California Palace of the Legion
   of Honor (SF) 38
California Science Center 34
California State Capitol 46-7
California State Railroad
   Museum 47
Calistoga 30
CalTrain 111
Campanile (LA) 72-3
camping 106
Canter's (LA) 72
car rental 113
car travel, *see* driving
Carmel-by-the-Sea 27, 81,
   105, 70
Carnelian Room (SF) 90
Cartoon Art Museum 38
Casting Couch (SF) 92
Cat & Fiddle (LA) 86
Catalina, *see* Santa Catalina
   Island
Catalina Bar & Grill (LA) 86
Cha Cha Cha (SF) 76
chemists, *see* pharmacies
Chez Panisse 74
Chiat-Day Building 12
children 48-9
Chinatown (LA) 19, 72
Chinatown (SF) 37, 53
Chinese Culture Center (SF) 57
Chinois on Main (LA) 73
cinemas, *see* film
City Hall (LA) 18
City Lights (SF) 66
Civic Center (SF) 39
Civic Center (LA) 18
classical music, *see* music

Clay Theatre (SF) 92
Cliff House (SF) 39
climate 108
clothing 61, 66
Club Bombay (SD) 96
Club Deluxe (SF) 91
Coachella Valley 70
Cobb's Comedy Club (SF) 89
CoCo Club (SF) 93
Coit Tower (SF) 39
Columbia 44
Comedy & Magic Club (LA) 85
Comedy Store (LA) 85
Comedy Store (SD) 95
comedy venues 85-6, 89, 95
Conga Room (LA) 86
consulates 113-14
credit cards 114
Croce's Top Hat Bar & Grill
   (SD) 95
Curran Theater (SF) 89
customs 110

D
Dakota Grill & Spirits (SD) 78
dance 12
dance clubs 86-7, 90-91
David's Place (SD) 79
Death Valley 16
Del Norte Redwoods SP 25
dentists 117
department stores 61, 65
Derby, The (LA) 86
Detour, The (SF) 93
disabled travellers 119
discos, *see* dance clubs
Disneyland 17
diving 51
DL Bliss SP 24
Dodger Stadium (LA) 88
Dragonfly (LA) 86-7
Dresden Room (LA) 86
drinks, *see* liquor
driving 112-13
duty free 110

E
economy 9
Egyptian Theater (LA) 36
El Capitan Theater (LA) 36
El Pueblo de Los Angeles 19
El Sombrero (LA) 74
electricity 115
email 116
embassies, *see* consulates

sights index